HOW TO: CATHOLIC FAMILY

Nurturing Faith in the Messiness of Everyday Life

TOMMY & KAREN TIGHE

Published by The Word Among Us Press
7115 Guilford Drive, Suite 100
Frederick, Maryland 21704
wau.org

23 22 21 20 19   1 2 3 4 5

ISBN: 978-1-59325-350-9

Cover design by Faceout Studios, Derek Thornton

Made and printed in the United States of America

Library of Congress Control Number: 2018967881

Acknowledgments

We can only hope that this book is as much fun to read as it was to write.

Doing a project together was such a blessing for us, and we feel grateful for the opportunity to have worked on it with the lovely team at The Word Among Us Press. First and foremost, we have to thank Beth McNamara, the publisher of the Press. Beth reached out to us and asked if we had any interest in writing this book, even though we're seriously unqualified, and she helped us every single step of the way.

Next, we have to thank our children: James, Paul, Andrew, and Luke. If it weren't for these loving, beautiful children, where would we have gotten all the great stories for this book? They constantly surprise us with their love, inspire us to be better, and put up with us even though we're so far from perfect.

Luke, our fourth son, who died shortly after his birth in 2016, has touched us in a different way, showing us the path to unconditional love and bringing us closer to the Lord than we ever could have imagined. In his short life, he taught us how to love, and he continues to guide us to love the Lord with all our hearts, so that we can be open to all God has for us.

And thank you to all of you, the readers of this book! We hope that you have some fun and will find at least a couple of our ideas interesting and helpful enough to give them a shot in your own family.

TABLE OF CONTENTS

INTRODUCTION

We rushed from the minivan into Mass, genuflected before stuffing ourselves into the front pew, and felt quite an immense sense of accomplishment because the priest was still walking down the aisle. Successfully getting a family with three young children to Mass on time feels like winning the gold medal of Catholic parenting.

It was only during the second reading that we noticed that our eight-year-old had oatmeal all over his face, our five-year-old was wearing two left shoes, and our three-year-old was holding two "swords" that he had made with K'nex prior to leaving the house.

Well, at least we made it on time, right?

When the Word Among Us asked if we would work together on a how-to book to help families lead a faith-filled and faith-focused life, we had the obvious reaction: what in the world could we possibly offer others trying to grow in their Catholic faith as a family?! That question seemed like a great place to start

Raising a family while striving to pass on a love for the Catholic faith can feel like trying to build a plane while you're flying it. We catch ourselves making things up as we go along, trying our best to get things right, and most often reflecting at the end of the day on all the ways we failed to meet our unrealistically high expectations. This humbling reality seemed like another great place to start.

In his Second Letter to the Corinthians, St. Paul reminds us of something we so often forget while we're mired in recurring thoughts about our failures as parents:

"My grace is sufficient for you, for power is made perfect in weakness." I will rather boast most gladly of my weaknesses, in order that the power of Christ may dwell with me. Therefore, I am content with weaknesses, insults, hardships, persecutions, and constraints, for the sake of Christ; for when I am weak, then I am strong. (2 Corinthians 12:9-10)

So take heart, fellow weak Catholic parents, as you pray for strength in the face of tantrums, diapers, and battles over eating all the veggies on the plate. God is closer than you think. As you lie in bed at night reviewing the times you have fallen short, make an effort to remember that God will reveal his strength in your weakness.

Easier said than done, right?

This book is a journey into the heart of a Catholic family trying to make sense of the suffering but always taking time to be joyful and silly—even when we're late for Mass. Through it all—the baths, meals, school, homework, random wardrobe changes, stepping on Legos, tucking kids into bed fourteen times per night, folding piles of laundry, picking up the house—we make an effort to incorporate the beauty and importance of our Catholic faith.

Are you ready for some hilarious stories? Are you ready for some helpful ideas? Are you ready to tuck the kids into bed, pray they don't wake up fifteen minutes later, pour yourself a margarita, and settle in to learn some tips about how to bring Catholicism into your family's day-to-day life?

If so, let's begin!

ONE

DO AS I SAY *AND* AS I DO

Nourishing your own faith is integral to passing it on to your children.

Neither of us will ever forget the night that we were awake in the wee hours of the morning with our firstborn. Karen was vacuuming, and Tommy had two-month-old James strapped into his car seat, swinging it back and forth in order to lull the baby to sleep. This was supposed to work. It was in the parenting book, and we had tried absolutely everything else.

We looked at each other and burst into tears. We were failing miserably, and it was only the beginning of our parenting life. *This* was supposed to be the easy part, or so we thought. But the tough nights and inconsistent sleep went on month after month, until the "baby" was about two and a half.

Before we had James, we were the perfect parents. We had read all the books, knew all the answers, and had heaps of patience. But everything we thought we knew about parenthood suddenly seemed irrelevant when James arrived. Like most new parents, we were terrified to even walk out of the hospital with that tiny baby.

If ever there was a baby who caused his parents to eat humble pie, James was it. He fussed a lot, hardly napped, and was a restless sleeper during the night—every night. We found ourselves struggling to be the parents we thought we should be. And we were *exhausted*. We didn't have the right answer for how to soothe him. We didn't have the right answer for how to get him to sleep. We didn't have the right answer for anything.

Our parenting has evolved as we've added to the family and the kids have gotten older—being parents has become both easier and harder with each milestone and year that passes. The perfect answers never seem to come at just the right time—when we realize something has got to change, we find ourselves learning the hard way, through trial and error.

Our kids often seem to learn the same way. Fast-forward a few years, when James was about three and our second son, Paul, was a wee six months. It was a busy time! One evening Karen was cooking in the kitchen while the kids played at her feet. "Don't touch the stove," she warned James. "It's hot."

As you can probably guess, James waddled over, put his hand directly on the stove, and lightly burned his fingertips. Immediately Karen felt both sorrow for her hurt child and frustration that he didn't listen to her warning. She tried to gently explain that she told him not to touch the stove for his own good. "Mommy gives you these rules so that you don't hurt yourself or someone else. You need to listen to what I say even if you don't understand why."

And then it hit her: her explanation to James applied to herself in regard to the Church. Karen had been struggling with certain Church teachings but hadn't considered that those teachings establish boundaries that protect us. We should do our best to follow them, even if we don't fully understand—just as James failed to understand why Karen warned him about the hot stove.

When it comes to taking a look at ourselves in the mirror and assessing our own faith, things can get uncomfortable. It's much more comfortable to look at our *families* as the thing we need to fix when we're looking for ways to live a more intentionally Catholic family life. But we have to take a step back, pause, and recognize that we might need to change something within *ourselves* first. If we want to impart the importance and the beauty of the Catholic faith to our children, if we have any real interest in living an authentically Catholic life at home and in the world, we have to start with ourselves.

Are we still beginners despite having the *Catechism* pounded into our heads since before we could walk? Are we walking the walk but not really pushing ourselves to go deeper? Or on the other hand, are we ready to run an RCIA class and help inspire others to grow in their relationship with Christ and his Church? We'll never know unless we take the time to slow down, pause, and reflect.

Assessing Your Prayer Life

We all want our kids to see the power of prayer in their lives, starting from an early age. We take the time to practice the Hail Mary with them. We make sure they don't sneak a bite before we finish our prayer before meals. We never fail to end the bedtime routine with a prayer before they close their eyes. And while all of that is important, our children are always keeping a close eye on *us,* to examine what kind of prayer life *we* have. They look to us to quench their curiosity when it comes to what it means to pray as an adult, as a parent, and as a spouse.

Clare Anderson and Joanna Bogle, in their book *John Paul II, Man of Prayer*, provide a beautiful glimpse of the power of a good example when they speak of the prayer life of the future pope's father:

> Prayer was a constant in their lives; the Captain prayed often during the day, on his knees. The two read the Bible and prayed the rosary together. Sometimes the young boy would wake in the night and see his father kneeling in the dark, praying silently.[1]

All of us should regularly assess where we are in our prayer life: Do we pray every day? Do we pray spontaneously as we go through the day? Do we thank God for our blessings?

If we can answer yes to each of these questions, chances are we're in a good place in terms of prayer. We ought to reevaluate our prayer life often, however, so that we don't slip into a lazy relationship with God. If we answer no to one (or all) of these questions, then how do we start to move in the right direction?

How Can a Parent Find Time to Pray Every Day?

We hear over and over again that it's important to pause and spend time in conversation with the Lord every day. We know it's true and feel an inner turmoil when we go through a day (or a week . . . or more) without praying. But how is a parent supposed to find time to pray each day?

Seriously.

If your family is anything like ours, your children are up and ready to rock and roll before you get a chance to wipe the sleep from your eyes. You don't need an alarm clock because, without fail, before the sun begins to peek into your backyard, your children are jumping on your bed asking you which superhero you'll pretend to be that day. (You're inevitably going to pick the wrong one, by the way.) From that moment forward, the day is a nonstop event.

It can seem as if we don't have a spare moment to make the Sign of the Cross, let alone engage with God in a spontaneous and fruitful conversation. Sure, the kids eventually go to bed, and we might have an hour or two before we too crash. But by that point, we're so worn out that we lack the mental capacity to offer up a few words to the creator of the universe.

What's the solution?

Well, we can start by expanding our understanding of what it means to pray. As Catholics, we often think of prayer as a big event, a time set aside to go into our rooms, take out our rosaries, and meditate on the Glorious Mysteries for thirty minutes. If we don't have a huge chunk of time on our hands, we figure that we don't have enough time to pray.

It doesn't have to be this way.

Mother Angelica, the well-known Poor Clare sister who founded the EWTN Television and Radio Network, shared a technique on one of her shows that helps to expand our understanding of prayer. Whenever something good happens, *no matter how mildly good it is*, quickly and immediately thank Jesus. The traffic light stays green longer than you expected, allowing you to make it through safely? Thank you, Jesus. The printer at work successfully prints out the spreadsheet you've been working on? Thank you, Jesus. The microwave heats up your food perfectly on the first try? Thank you, Jesus.

There needn't be pomp and circumstance around our prayer life. Simply staying focused on the fact that everything good comes from Jesus can help us to stay the course throughout our day. And consistently thanking Jesus throughout our day prepares us for all the negativity that is waiting around the corner. When we spend our entire day with Jesus on our mind, we tend to be less troubled by the anxieties and problems that inevitably surface.

The Jesus Prayer is another quick way to keep your prayer life going throughout the day. This short and to-the-point invocation has long been popular in the Eastern Church and has gained ground in the West as well:

"Lord Jesus Christ, Son of God, have mercy on me, a sinner."
That's it. So much power packed in that one tiny statement. Repeating this brief prayer as we go about the day can totally turn things around. As we admit our need for God's mercy and help, the prayer reminds us to rely on him for the solutions to our struggles.

Setting Aside Some Quiet Time

That being said, in order to build our relationship with the Lord and also to avoid feeling drained, we have to incorporate quality quiet time in our days, time when we can listen to God in the silence and allow the Spirit to move us in the direction of God's will. Those moments can be few and precious for parents, and might require getting creative in order to make them happen.

As odd as it might seem, the bathroom can often provide this silent solace. If we fight off the urge to scroll on our phones while we're in there and embrace the time, instead, as an opportunity to be alone in quiet conversation with the Lord, we might find a key to getting that time in the midst of a busy day.

Of course, even the bathroom might not be a safe space with kids around. When we're in the bathroom, our kids spend most of the time either banging on the door, fighting, or feeling comfortable just walking right in. And so when the bathroom doesn't provide the privacy we need, we look elsewhere for little moments of silence. Those moments when the kids are enthralled in a video, for example, or when they're outside and the windows are shut tight, blocking out the screaming, or the little bit of time between when they fall asleep and we collapse into bed—all of these can be opportunities to pause, reflect, reset, and allow the Lord to speak to us.

Getting in Touch with the Bible

Some of our quiet time with the Lord should include time reading Scripture. We speak from experience when we say that this isn't necessarily the first thing Catholics think of when they think about praying.

A few years ago, we were going through some challenges, and even though the need for prayer was growing, it was flat-out difficult to pray. Karen had a deep love of the Rosary, but now her go-to prayer felt like a chore. As God seemed to drift farther and farther away, she felt the need to reach out and bring the words of Jesus into her life. So while going through the nightly struggle of rocking a reluctant one-year-old to sleep, she decided to go through different books of the Bible using a Catholic app on her smartphone. She started with the Gospels, moved on to the Acts of the Apostles, and then started scrolling through the various letters of St. Paul.

Tommy, meanwhile, was sitting on the couch in the living room, scrolling through Twitter. Karen wins.

After a few weeks of going through each Gospel this way, Karen came out one night after putting the baby to bed and said, "You know what? I actually know *way* more of the Bible than I thought I did."

This is because Catholics have a secret weapon when it comes to experiencing the Bible: the Mass. Every Sunday, during the Liturgy of the Word, we hear readings from the Bible: first a reading from the Old Testament (usually), next a Psalm, then a reading from a New Testament writing, and finally a reading from one of the Gospels.

In addition, nearly the entire Mass features words taken directly from Scripture. "Hosanna in the highest"? Yep (Mark 11:10). "Lamb of God, who takes away the sin of the world"? Most definitely (John 1:29). "Lord, I am not worthy to have you enter under my roof"? You had better believe it (Matthew 8:8)! And plenty more. We're being spoon-fed sacred Scripture on the regular without even realizing it.

Once we take the time to start going through the Bible for our own spiritual growth, it all clicks into place. Because of the Mass, we are more familiar with the Bible than we might realize, and that can give us a sense of comfort when we dive into the word. Also, Karen's adventure with her smartphone, in the rocking chair with our sweet little fuss-bucket, showed us that we're walking around with the Bible in our pockets all day long, and hadn't realized it.

Most of our smartphones give us access not only to the Bible but also to various Catholic apps packed with prayers, including litanies and novenas. And even if we don't download one of those apps, we've got access to the Internet in the palm of our hand. The whole Bible is sitting out there waiting for us to read it in our downtime. When we find ourselves pulling out our phone to do random reading, maybe we could steer clear of Facebook and Twitter every once in a while in favor of jumping into the Letter to the Hebrews to see what God wants to share with us that day.

Going beyond Memorized Prayers

After dear Protestant friends of ours had their first baby, we went to their home to meet the new bundle of joy. The baby was about a month old and was fussy and restless. His mom explained that he had been having some tummy troubles that made him uncomfortable.

We sat down for dinner, and the husband started to say grace, but it wasn't the grace *we* were used to. It was a spontaneous prayer of thanks followed by an intention the likes of which we'd never heard before: "Thank you, Jesus, for the gift of this day, this delicious meal. And, Jesus, please take the baby's gas away. In Jesus's name. Amen." We shared a quick glance of shock. Did he really say "gas" to Jesus?! It felt a little awkward to our Catholic-since-birth ears.

We Catholics turn to traditional memorized prayers more often than we reach out to God in our own words. The prayers we memorized when young are powerful, of course, especially in times of crisis when we can't seem to find the words we're looking for. It's consoling and beautiful to be able to jump right into a Hail Mary, a Memorare, and even a quick Glory Be. But spontaneous prayer can underscore that we truly understand we are a people in relationship to Christ, that we are a part of his family, and that we believe he cares about what is going on in our lives at any given moment.

Spontaneous prayer can take some serious effort for Catholics—it doesn't seem to come as naturally to us as it does to our non-Catholic friends—but it is another way for us to draw closer to God, increasing our intimacy with him.

The Couple That Prays Together . . .

At the Engaged Encounter retreat we attended before walking down the aisle, the presenters suggested that we start now to develop a prayer life together. Tommy was downright frightened by this idea. Growing up as an only child, he experienced prayer as something very private. The idea of welcoming another person, even his wife, into that private world made him feel too vulnerable. We tried, and it felt clunky, so we kind of gave up.

We didn't give it much thought until we went through a molar pregnancy—a nonviable pregnancy that results in a rapidly growing benign uterine tumor. Not only was there no baby to celebrate, as we thought, but Karen would have to undergo two surgeries to remove the tumor, and there was a risk of it regrowing and metastasizing. We were completely wrecked, but we were wrecked together; we felt there was nowhere else to turn but to God.

We prayed a novena to St. Jude together every night during the pregnancy, and it felt *so* good. We felt more connected to each other, more connected to God, and we really felt the Lord moving in our life.

After the period of suffering passed, however, we fell back into our old habits. We continue to try to come up with ways to pray together and have found a few that hit the mark. But it's hard work!

One practice that has helped us open up in prayer and grow closer to each other is praying for each other with each other. For example, Tommy prays an Our Father aloud, Karen prays a Hail Mary aloud, Tommy thanks God for Karen and asks him to take care of her in a specific way, and Karen does the same for Tommy. Not only does this open us up to God's grace and power in our lives, but many, many times it has confirmed how in tune we are with each other's needs. When we spontaneously pray for something on behalf of the other, we can feel the concern and care we have for each other, that we're aware of one another's needs and struggles. We feel truly loved.

Confession

Tommy still remembers his first confession. He stood in line with the other kids, silently panicking over what was about to happen. As he approached the front of the line, he waited for the teacher to look away and then stealthily slid to the end of the line to buy more time. In the end, the experience was far less traumatic than anticipated, but that sense of anxiety while waiting in line for confession and even just *thinking* about going to Confession has hung around for him.

Don't get us wrong; nothing beats that feeling when you're walking out of the confessional, that feeling of a weight lifted off your shoulders. It's great! But the anxiety of sharing our deepest and darkest failings with a priest, even anonymously through the screen, can keep us away from the healing power of this sacrament for far too long.

How long has it been since you've been to Confession? For many of us, it's been too long, and so we aren't tapping into the grace that would help free us from our sins and help us grow in holiness.

But let's be real: the confessional isn't always a fun place to be. Some of us who have been Catholic for a while have had experiences there that have made us want to avoid it. But even if you have had a less than perfect experience—a penance that didn't seem right, for example, or a confessor who glossed over a serious sin when you were hoping to get guidance—you can talk about that with a priest who can help you find your way back into this source of healing and peace.

So where's the hope? Where's the motivation? What can we do to open ourselves up to going to confession more frequently? What can we do to better prepare for a good confession? What can we do to make progress in this part of our spiritual journey?

The first step is realizing what Confession means for us and what it can do for us here on our journey. According to the *Catechism of the Catholic Church:*

> "The whole power of the sacrament of Penance consists in restoring us to God's grace and joining us with him in an intimate friendship." Reconciliation with God is thus the purpose and effect of this sacrament. For those who receive the sacrament of Penance with contrite heart and religious disposition, reconciliation "is usually followed by peace

and serenity of conscience with strong spiritual consolation." Indeed the sacrament of Reconciliation with God brings about a true "spiritual resurrection," restoration of the dignity and blessings of the life of the children of God, of which the most precious is friendship with God. (*CCC,* 1468, quoting *Roman Catechism,* II, V, 18; Council of Trent; cf. Luke 15:32)

As we come face-to-face with Jesus in this sacrament and receive his forgiveness, we open ourselves to deepen our friendship with him.

We once attended a talk given by a Dominican priest who then heard confessions afterward. It had been a long time for Karen, and she was nervous about going. But then the priest said something that put her at ease. He urged everyone to remember that there is no judgment in the confessional, only God's mercy.

Examination of Conscience

The best way to make a good confession is to prayerfully consider the things you've done that cut you off from God and other people. You might want to make a list, because it can be hard to recall all the ways you've failed to live a good Christian life since your last confession. Enter the examination of conscience, a means of reviewing our lives and looking for ways to improve.

It's been recommended by saints through the ages, such as St. Ignatius of Loyola, St. Francis de Sales, and St. Teresa of Calcutta.

There are different ways to approach this practice, but pointed questions that get straight to the heart of what we should and should not be doing are a great way to keep track of our spiritual progress and our obedience to the vows or requirements of our state in life.

The United States Conference of Catholic Bishops (USCCB) provides a great examination of conscience for married Catholics that cuts to the chase and helps us openly and honestly examine our lives.

> Have I gone to Mass every Sunday? Have I participated at Mass, or have I daydreamed or been present with a blank mind?
> Have I prayed every day (fifteen to twenty minutes)?
> Have I read the Bible? Have I studied the truths of our faith and allowed them to become more part of the way I think and act? Have I read any spiritual books or religious literature? . . .

> Have I cared for my spouse? Have I been generous with my time? Have I been affectionate and loving? Have I told my spouse that I love him or her?
> Have I been concerned about the spiritual well-being of my spouse?
> Have I listened to my spouse? Have I paid attention to his or her concerns, worries, and problems? Have I sought these out?
> Have I allowed resentments and bitterness toward my spouse to take root in my mind? Have I nurtured these? Have I forgiven my spouse for the wrongs he or she has committed against me? . . .

Have I cared for the spiritual needs of my children? Have I been a shepherd and guardian as God has appointed me? Have I tried to foster a Christian family where Jesus is Lord? Have I taught my children the Gospel and the commandments of God?

Have I prayed with them?

Have I been persistent and courageous in my training and teaching? Have I disciplined them when necessary? Have I been lazy and apathetic?

Have I talked with them to find out their problems, concerns, and fears? Have I been affectionate toward them? Have I hugged them and told them that I love them? Have I played or recreated with them?[2]

These are the types of questions we can ask ourselves in order to become more aware of our faults and failings and make a serious push to improve in those areas. Is it intimidating to do this? Yes. Will it help us to make better confessions and thus open ourselves up to a better relationship with God? Definitely.

Speaking of Mass

If we want to intentionally live the life of a Catholic family, we must begin with "the source and summit of the Christian life," the Holy Eucharist.[3] Consistent attendance at Mass on Sundays and holy days of obligation is an absolute must for Catholic parents—not only because it's a sin to miss Mass without a serious reason but also because it sets things in motion for living out our faith the rest of the week. Just because we're supposed to, however, doesn't mean that it's easy.

Making it to Mass with kids can be a real struggle. Sometimes it seems as if Jesus would totally understand that your kids would be absolute terrors in the pews that day, and so you have to skip Mass. The fact that many parishes aren't explicitly welcoming to families—and in reality some parishes seem downright hostile—compounds the feeling that it's better to avoid Mass when the kids are less than angelic.

As a Church, we can't allow families to feel left out. Pope Francis has reminded us that "the family is the cradle of life."[4] If we somehow make that cradle of life feel unwelcome at Mass, we are doing something seriously wrong. Regardless of less than favorable circumstances, it's our responsibility as parents to take our kids to Mass.

Now, some of you may be on a slow journey back to faith or struggling with situations that are out of your control. It's worth pointing out here that Jesus always meets us where we are, and he stands with us, ready to help us take small steps forward in our journey with him. Rather than feel like a failure if your family only makes it to Mass once a month, discuss your situation with a priest in Confession as you try to make your way forward. Sure, you see your Catholic friends posting cute pictures on social media of their families all dressed up every week looking like it's so darn easy, but if you're in a place where making it once a month is the best you can do, that's where you'll need to start. Try going every other week as you take steps toward the goal of attending each week.

Listening, Reading, and Watching the Faith

Tommy went quite a while without knowing that Catholic radio existed. He owes his discovery to the fact that he experienced a transition at work that led to a lot of downtime. To this day, he's not sure why, but he took out his smartphone (a Palm Pre, at the time, if anyone remembers that piece of junk), clicked on a very archaic TuneIn Radio app, and searched for "Catholic." Tommy can trace his wholehearted embrace of the faith to that exact moment.

Up until then, he was a cradle Catholic who had been going through the motions for the majority of his life. Sure, he continued going to Mass every Sunday throughout his wild ride at UC Santa Barbara, but he wasn't really engaged with the faith. And he definitely wasn't embracing all the things that the Catholic Church teaches. Catholic radio changed all that.

Tommy stumbled very quickly on two shows that changed his life: EWTN's *Open Line* and *Catholic Answers Live*. These two radio shows, completely ordinary in format, became his gateway back into the full banquet of the Church. The shows' hosts and guests answered questions he'd always had, and after a short time, *he* knew the answers, knew the persuasive arguments, and even knew the chapters and verses to back it all up.

Imagine that! A cradle Catholic who knows a thing or two about the faith. And he owes it all to the jump start that Catholic radio gave him. It's still the only thing blasting from the speakers during his morning and afternoon commutes (unless, of course, he's in need of some straight-up '90s hip-hop . . . you can't deny that urge). All these years later, it remains a source of truth, comfort, and guidance on his spiritual journey.

There is so much to learn about Catholicism that it can feel like we're never going to know it all. *Spoiler alert: We're never going to know it all—at least not this side of heaven.* However, we are so blessed to live at a time when the information we want and need is right at our fingertips—Catholic radio, books, podcasts, websites, YouTube accounts, blogs, magazines, apps, online question-and-answer resources, and more! The Catholic Church has made gigantic strides in getting everything we need to know about our faith out there, waiting for us.

TWO

WERE THERE DINOSAURS ON THE ARK?

The importance of faith conversations with children, even at a young age

Kids are always asking questions. Why do I have to eat this? Why does *he* get more than *me*? Why can't I stay up late and watch cartoons and eat ice cream and go to the store without shoes? Why? Why?? Why?!?!

When James was a toddler, it became clear to us that the way he learned most of what he knew was by proposing an endless series of "why" questions. It would get tiresome trying to answer them all, and usually, after two or three whys in a row, we would cut off the line of questioning with either "Because that's how it is" or "Well, James, . . . I just don't know."

One day forever stands out in Karen's mind as the day of a thousand questions. She decided that rather than blow off

James' questions, she would make an effort to give some kind of answer to even the toughest and strangest of them, regardless of how much or how little she knew. Karen and James were headed to meet up with some friends about twenty miles away, and the questioning started as they backed down our driveway.

James pointed to a large piece of construction machinery in our neighbor's yard and asked, "What is that?" Karen didn't know *what* it was exactly, but she gave it a shot and answered the question as honestly as she could. "It looks like a machine Jim is going to use to rip up their yard."

"Why do they rip up the yard?"

Then she noticed a large pipe lying in the neighbor's front yard along with this hunk of machinery and said, "Look, there's a pipe there. They probably need to replace a pipe that goes to their house, so they need this machine to dig a hole for it."

"But why?"

Karen was not well versed in pipe replacement, but she did her best. "Well, sometimes a big tree root will grow so large that it will actually grow into a pipe that's buried in the ground, and the pipe will break, and sometimes it'll have to be replaced."

"But why would the pipe be buried in the ground if a tree could grow in it?"

Karen continued to answer each of James' subsequent questions, and it became a fun game to see where the line of questioning would go. As soon as Karen finished answering one question, James would immediately ask another. And on and on it went for the entire twenty-minute ride. They discussed a range of topics, from home maintenance to international travel and how trees are made into paper.

As they approached their destination, James asked one last question that Karen stumbled over: "But if Aunt Maureen is an adult, why does she live at Grandma and Grandpa's house?" Despite knowing that James was too young to understand the state of the economy and Aunt Maureen's hard work to eventually get out on her own, Karen gave in, let out a big sigh, and said, "Some things are a mystery."

This short ride changed the way Karen approached James' budding curiosity in everything. Not that anything they talked about that day was significant, but it hit Karen that everything James knew (more or less) had come from what she and Tommy had taught him. And he was eager to hear what we had to say. James asked us questions and listened to us as if we actually had the answers to anything that he could ever ask. This left Karen in awe of how precious his little mind was and how much he was ready to absorb.

Over time our kids have gone from the typical kid-level questions right into epic questions, like "Why does God let people make bad choices?" and "Why would some of the angels decide to go against God?" and even the dreaded "*Why* do we believe (insert any Catholic teaching)?" These moments always give us pause as parents and sometimes leave us scrambling to come up with the "right" answer. We start sweating, panicking, assuming that if we don't provide the perfect answer in that moment, our kids are going to go off to college, become heretics, and join some cult waiting for the return of an alien named Gorg. And it will all be because we couldn't come up with an answer to the question of why there were no dinosaurs on the ark.

Imagine!

The Why, Not Just the What

When we look back on the faith instruction our parents handed down to us, we recognize that they frequently gave us the "what" of Catholic teaching but far less often offered the "why" behind that teaching. We knew we should help the poor, but we weren't well versed in the long tradition of Catholic social teaching or the spirituality behind it. We knew we were expected to attend Mass every Sunday and on holy days of obligation, but we didn't understand why it was such a serious matter to skip without a good reason. We knew we were supposed to save sex for marriage, but we didn't comprehend the beauty behind this teaching.

We don't fault our parents; it can be hard to explain complicated Church teaching to kids, especially when they're teenagers and only half paying attention. But we stumbled upon the *why* behind all of these teachings only when we were well into our twenties. We realized that for us, the whys—the reasons we were being asked to believe and do certain things as Catholics—were the keys to unlocking understanding, acceptance, and zeal for the teachings of the Church.

So now that we're parents, we're always quick to explain the *why* after we explain the *what*, right? Well, . . . not exactly. It's hard!

Part of the issue is that the faith of young kids is incredible. They take the most complicated mysteries of the faith and accept them as if they were being told the sky is blue. God is truly present in that tiny little wafer? Sure, makes sense. The saints in heaven care about us, are aware of what's happening on earth, and intercede on our behalf? Sounds right. This is why Jesus told us that we should have a childlike faith: *it's the kind of faith that saves.*

Just because our kids accept the teachings of the Church wholeheartedly, however, doesn't mean we're off the hook when it comes to exploring and explaining the whys behind them. Keep in mind that some aspects of faith are and always will be a mystery (how Jesus becomes present in the Eucharist at the words of consecration, for example), but there is still much we can learn, even about the mysteries. The whys are what carry us through. The whys are what help us cling to truth when tested and tempted by other ideas. The whys are really, *really* important.

If our kids can hang on to the *why*s as they grow up, they might be better able to avoid some of the mistakes many of us made along the way after receiving only the *what*s.

Sparking a Conversation with Your Kids

But having a conversation with kids about anything, let alone about questions of faith, isn't necessarily easy! As we sit around the dinner table as a family each night, for example, we always try to engage our kids in conversation about their day. James usually isn't super interested. "Nothing, really" is the typical response when we ask what he did that day. We press on: "What did you do during recess? How about P.E.? Did you learn any cool new science facts?!" "Not really. Just a regular day."

We get annoyed about the lack of info, he gets annoyed by our constant demands for more info, and 'round and 'round we go. Tommy tries to slip in some clever communications techniques from his work as a marriage and family therapist, but as James continues to stonewall, it can be tempting to drop the conversation, drop the constant attempts to pull something (*anything*) out of our son. But we persist because these discussions about our days are important.

Just as important are conversations about the faith with our kids. And yet for some reason, we find that these conversations don't come naturally. Maybe it's because we're nervous they'll ask something we can't answer. Maybe it's because we're scared they won't know as much as they should at their age. Maybe it's because we're afraid of being exposed as failures. Maybe it's because we didn't have that kind of opportunity with our own parents. But it's *so* important.

Conversations are tools for education. Kids will be more open and learn far more from their parents when they can have an easygoing back-and-forth with them. They're far less interested when we try to drive home a point by way of a college-level lecture before tucking them into bed.

Maybe sparking those conversations doesn't have to be as intimidating as we make them out to be in our minds. It can be as simple as "What did you hear that you remember from Mass this morning?" or "What do you think about Jesus feeding all those people with so little food?" to "Do you have any questions about anything that you saw at Mass today?"

If that still seems intimidating, remember that the best way to spark a conversation with your kids about the faith is to live the faith in front of them. If you take time out of your Saturday to go to Confession, your kids are going to ask about it. If you pack up the whole family to help distribute gifts to the less fortunate around Christmastime, your kids are going to want an explanation for why they had to do that. When they see you living the faith, they'll want to know why. What inspires you? Why is it important? Should they be doing it too?

And just like that, you're on your way to helping them grow and foster their love of the Church Jesus founded.

Learning Together

When he was seven years old, James asked why some of the angels followed Satan in turning away from God if they were in heaven before making that choice. Why would they choose to be bad despite being face-to-face with God from the time of their creation, seeing him in all his beauty and majesty? We sat there staring off into space thinking, "Yeah, why *would* they do that?!"

These kinds of questions can be conversational stumbling blocks, as we've seen, because as parents, we often feel we're *supposed* to have all the answers. After all, when we look back on our own childhood, it seems that our parents knew it all. So shouldn't we know it all?

Well, in reality, they didn't know everything (sorry, Mom and Dad). And we can't expect to either, especially when it comes to questions about faith.

The Internet can be a big asset here. When your kids start asking questions you can't answer, you can find much of the information you need through the amazing Catholic resources online. Don't be afraid to tell your kids that you'll investigate and get back to them—but make sure you do.

When your kids are old enough, you can sit down together at the computer to research answers to their questions. Even to do that, however, you'll have to do some work ahead of time. You'll want to find and bookmark sites that are kid- and teen-friendly, faithful to Church teaching, and safe. You don't want to be randomly scrolling through the Web looking for answers and finding who knows what.

Sure, it would feel good to know the answers off the top of your head when kids ask questions, but doing the research together and discussing the answers can help them make the material their own. It also will contribute to the sort of open communication about faith-related questions that we've discussed in this chapter, serving you well as your kids get into their teen and young adult years. Bottom line: finding the right answer, either through your own research or together, is way better than responding to a question with "Because he's God, and he can do whatever he wants."

But Some of What They
Think Is So Darn Cute!

Kids think deep thoughts. You don't have to hang around them very long to discover this. They often approach their parents with questions about the faith, but they're also constantly trying to work things out in their own heads when it comes to life's mysteries. And to be fair, they come up with some pretty awesome explanations.

One of our kids surmised that St. Michael was his guardian angel because he saw a stained glass window depicting St. Michael holding a sword made out of fire, and how absolutely cool is a sword made out of fire?!?! It simply *had* to be true that St. Michael was his guardian angel. His idea certainly was cute. That's why it was hard to decide if we should tell him the difference among the angels—some being guardian angels, some archangels, and so on. Should we parents burst our kids' bubbles when they come up with a notion about the faith that may be a tad off?

What if their idea isn't essential to the faith, such as our son laying claim to St. Michael? What if their thinking is way too cute to correct? This is a tough area for parents. On the one hand, for example, what's the harm in our children thinking people become angels when they die? But on the other hand, you want to hand down the truths of the faith from the beginning so that your kids don't end up questioning more essential items along the way.

The trick is to correct with gentleness and kindness. Let's take the example of people becoming angels when they die. It sounds so nice: heaven filled with all the souls of the faithful departed, only now they have an awesome set of wings and other typical angelic items. It makes kids feel happy and at peace to think of all those angels in heaven watching over us. But the truth is that we *don't* become angels when we die.

The story doesn't end there, of course, because what we become is something even more exciting. We become what God destined us to be: great saints who sit before the throne of God and forever exist in the mind-blowing presence of his love, interceding for everyone who needs help down on earth and in purgatory.

As parents, we don't want to dash the dreams of our children, but we do want to show them that the truth may be even more exciting than what they dreamed up. We can be tempted to let kids believe something that isn't quite right, but kids are far more willing than adults to incorporate the truth into their thought process. The time to point them in the right direction is now.

Be Willing to Tell Your Kids That We're Different

It was Christmastime, and after bundling everyone up, we packed the kids into the van and drove through our neighborhood looking at the Christmas lights and decorations in people's yards. We have a couple of neighbors who go all out, and it's a fun tradition for the kids (and us too) to ooh and aah over their hard work. Of course, not everyone puts up lights, which sparked a question from our five-year-old: how come not everyone puts up lights?

We had an easy answer: not everyone celebrates Christmas. Then came the next logical questions: Why doesn't everyone celebrate Christmas? Don't they believe in God?

In his innocence, our son didn't know that there were people who don't believe in God or who aren't Christian. We live in a very diverse area, and still, the thought that other families might not be like our family was strange to him.

Once your kids hit school age, it's not going to be long before they realize something about being Catholic: we're different; some might even say weird. We don't eat meat on Fridays during Lent, we believe in the true presence of Christ in the Eucharist, we wear a cross of ashes on our foreheads on Ash Wednesday, and we ask the dead to pray for us. We're countercultural, and we owe it to our kids to let them know that up-front.

Being Catholic will inevitably lead to situations where they are singled out and made to feel "other." If your family doesn't eat meat on Friday, your child might be the only kid not joining in on Cheeseburger Friday in the cafeteria. Or your kids might be ignored or mocked because they're kind and considerate to the kid being bullied rather than joining the attack. Giving your kids a sense of what lies ahead will help them persevere as they live out the faith. In preparing them for this experience, you can share your own stories about being put under the spotlight because of your faith.

Tommy remembers an incident from middle school when this hit home for him. He had purchased a delicious smelling cheeseburger in the cafeteria without remembering that it was a Friday in Lent. As he pulled the foil back and drew the burger to his lips, a non-Catholic classmate (Tommy still remembers you, *Todd*) shouted from another table, "Hey! I thought Catholics weren't allowed to eat meat on Fridays."

It was like a punch to the gut. Tommy took a slow walk to the trash can to toss it as the classmate shouted after him, "You Catholics are so weird!" The insult didn't hurt as much as having to go hungry for the rest of the day, but the experience has always stuck with Tommy.

Speaking of Vocations . . .

One final thought as we consider conversations to have with our kids. Most of us, as parents, have a vocation to the married life. Our kids look at us, imagine what their future will be like, and what they see is family. They see the vocation of marriage. This is great—we're all for marriage—but will they ever give even the slightest thought to the ordained or religious life if we don't talk about these options as a family?

We are in the middle of a religious vocation crisis in the United States. Young people don't seem to be drawn to a life of poverty, chastity, and obedience in the way they seemingly were back in the good ol' days, and now we're left with a priest shortage. Don't even ask us the last time we saw a religious sister in person; it's been *way* too long.

Talk with your kids about the impact that priests and religious have had on your life growing up. Maybe stay away from the tired jokes about nuns smacking kids on their hands with rulers, and instead talk about the sister who helped you through a difficult time, the priest who helped you in the confession that brought you back to the Church and lifted a weight off your shoulders, or the religious brother who stood with you, side by side, helping the poor.

One way to make these vocations come to life for our kids is by hanging out with priests and religious as a family. Inviting priests, sisters, brothers, and consecrated virgins into our homes will help our kids get to know them and see their life choices as viable options. If we don't introduce our kids to these men and women who are leading radical lives devoted to Jesus and his Church, then our children might miss the quiet voice of God when he whispers his plans into their hearts.

Be Present

Being present to our children and alert to all their questions is difficult. There are so many things competing for our attention in today's world, and though we know we *should* give our children our full attention whenever we're with them, we have a hard time staying focused. There are work emails buzzing our cell phones at all hours, the ever-present wish for a conversation just between husband and wife, the never-ending list of household chores, and, of course, social media.

Being present, however, lets our children know that they are important to us and that we hear and respect their questions. We have to work hard as parents to fight the distractions that lead us to miss or overlook an important question about Our Lady, guardian angels, or why we have to go to Mass on a Thursday just because it's August 15.

Take stock of the distractions in your life, and make a serious effort to put the phone down, leave work at work, and give your kids the attention they deserve. It's so hard, but so worth it.

THREE

ONLY WELL-BEHAVED KIDS GET DONUTS

Attending Mass and helping children understand it

When James was just over two years old, we started down the well-traveled but often challenging path of potty training. Karen was pregnant with our next child, Paul, and we thought, "Hey, what have we got to lose? If it works, it's one less kid in diapers."

With two parents watching his every move and tracking all of his bathroom trips and jelly bean rewards, it didn't take long for James to catch on, and he graduated to big-boy undies before Paul arrived. When it was Paul's turn to potty train, it was even easier. He had an older sibling to watch and look up to, and he took to it like a champ. We would shrug when people asked what our secret was: the boys were easy, and we got lucky.

Our luck ran out when it was time to potty train our third son, Andrew. We used every means we could think of to get him interested in using the potty: We tried making it sound fun and exciting. We tried bribing with jelly beans, chocolate chips, and M&Ms. We tried Elmo books and videos about the potty. We even let him pick out some really cool, super-fun, exciting, and brand-new underwear. He still wasn't interested. He would wake up with a dry diaper and tell us when he was about to go, but he refused to use the potty.

We decided to leave him alone and let him tell us when the time was right. We waited and waited. Months and months passed, and we started to get anxious, wondering if he would *ever* want to learn.

So when Andrew finally told us one morning that he was ready to wear his undies and go in the potty, we were thrilled—except for the fact that it was Sunday morning. Sunday morning meant we were heading out the door for Mass, which meant an entire hour and more of high anxiety, wondering if he'd have an accident. But he was so excited and so willing that we decided to go for it. After all, he was older now, and he was a lot better at telling us when he had to go. It also seemed like our big chance! We were on the verge of being free from diapers for the rest of our lives (or until the next baby came).

Andrew got dressed in his really cool, super-fun, exciting, and brand-new underwear, and we headed out the door. We were still nervous, and we pestered him a thousand times about using the bathroom, all before the entrance hymn was finished. Then, halfway through the second reading, Paul announced that *he* had to go to the bathroom, so Paul and Tommy headed out.

At this moment, Andrew became hysterical and called for Tommy over and over. Karen tried calming him down, but he kept saying that he only wanted Daddy. Then, since he's a smart kid, he claimed that he *also* had to go to the bathroom, figuring, apparently, that he would get his way and join Daddy in the bathroom. So Karen told James that she would be right back, left James in the pew, and headed out the door.

In the women's room, Andrew made it clear that he was completely unsatisfied with Karen taking care of him, and he screamed for Tommy the entire time.

Meanwhile, James was sitting in the pew by himself, and now he realized *he* had to go to the bathroom. So as soon as Tommy and Paul came back to the pew, they were right back out the door, this time with James in tow. This was just as Karen and Andrew were coming in the opposite side of the pew.

As soon as Andrew realized that Tommy was leaving again, he threw his head back and became completely hysterical. Karen grabbed him and made another quick exit to catch up with the others at the back of the church. After all of the kids did their thing in the bathroom, the whole family settled back into the pew just in time for the consecration.

We glanced over at each other, sharing a look that said more than words: life with kids can be wild, unpredictable, and sometimes stressful. Looking back, we laugh at the craziness of that morning.

Yes, getting to Mass can be the stuff of nightmares for growing Catholic families. From the Mass-messing-up-the-nap-schedule predicament, to the why-do-I-have-to-go arguments, to the kids who are *so slow* at getting their shoes on even though they insist they can do it themselves, it can be a challenge getting the whole family to show up on time for the celebration of the source and summit of our faith.

On a recent Sunday morning, for example, Tommy asked Paul to find some comfy yet appropriate clothes and get dressed on his own. This would allow Mommy and Daddy some time to get ready. As we walked toward the front door to leave, Paul jumped out of his bedroom dressed in a Spiderman costume, mask included.

Thanks be to God, he left the web shooter in his room.

These little setbacks give us a chance to head back to the drawing board as we try to craft that perfect Sunday morning routine that will get us all showered, dressed, in the pew, and ready for action.

It's All about the Planning

Before having kids, we'd see families showing up on time for Mass in their cute Sunday best and assume it happened easily. After getting into that phase of life ourselves, we quickly realized that you don't show up together, on time, fully dressed, by accident. It takes planning, people!

It may seem like overkill, but planning as early as the night before can go a long way toward making the Sunday morning rush go more smoothly. Laying out clothing, putting the cereal boxes on the counter, and finding matching socks (or two socks of the same size for each kid) can improve your Sunday morning experience when it's game time.

Of course, there's always going to be something you didn't plan for: a three-year-old who doesn't want to wear *that* shirt, a five-year-old who decides he needs to sit on the toilet for fifteen minutes when Mass starts in ten minutes, a dead battery in the van because someone clicked on the light in the back, and nobody noticed until it was time to go. And all of that's okay. God's watching, and he gets it.

He gets that we're trying our best and that life's just that hard sometimes. That's why many parishes have later Mass times! Sure, you may not want to sit through that teen Mass at 6:00 p.m. on Sunday evening, but for the sake of your sanity, that may be the best available option.

If you *are* able to herd the cats into the van and get to Mass on time, there are a few things you can do to help make it a success for everyone, including the people sitting around you.

Appropriate Expectations

Yes, it would be nice if you were raising the next Mother Teresa or John Paul II, but even St. Maximilian Kolbe got in trouble as a kid (once by dropping a frog in his mom's soup, if we believe the stories we've heard). Most kids don't suddenly get a boost of patience and a spirit of silence and attentiveness just because they walked into church. Given that painful reality, it's important to let your children know your expectations ahead of time. You're the ones who know your kids, their attention spans, and their ability to sit quietly, and so you're the ones who can set realistic expectations based on your children's ages and developmental levels.

Maybe you start off with "Please remember to try your best to be quiet and respectful during the consecration," move on to "Please be sure to listen and be attentive throughout the Mass," and finally proceed to "You need to respond with the right responses at the right time, sing along, and join in with everyone as we praise the Lord."

One step at a time, though.

We have found that a quick and specific conversation about Mass behavior on the way to church goes a long way, compared to just telling our kids to "be good." It's only fair that we give them details about what we're expecting. That helps also, when we give them feedback after Mass about how they met or fell short of the expectations we had for them. But we must always be realistic and not try to force our kids to be saints, even if that's what the adults in nearby pews hope we've produced when they see us sliding into the pew next to them.

Those adults sitting nearby, though, can be a big help to young parents at Mass. All parents of young children carry church-specific fears within them: the fear of a critical glance, the fear of someone making a negative comment as you walk out, the fear of disrupting someone's moment of prayer. Adults who are at Mass without children should support those working hard to keep their kids focused and in line, even if their efforts fall short. A supportive smile can go a long way, and an offer to hold a baby so that a parent and their three-year-old can run off to the potty can go even further!

Be a Good Example

That's right, parents. If we want our kids to behave, pay attention, and participate in the Mass, that means *we* have to behave, pay attention, and participate in the Mass. No whispering about a text that just came through, no eye rolling about how awful it is that the lady in the pew ahead of you brought her Starbucks in and, most definitely, no sitting quietly while the cantor, with raised hand, is begging the congregation to join in the hymn.

Our kids are never going to do what we want them to do at Mass unless *we* do what we want them to do at Mass. That's hard. One of the most difficult things about being a parent who wants to raise kids to be good and holy adults is that we have to actually try harder to be good and holy adults. We have to pray the prayers, listen to the readings, and wish God's blessings on the people around us.

Our kids are watching.

Practice the Prayers in the Comfort of Your Home

After one particularly frustrating Mass, Karen had had it with the boys complaining the whole hour about how long everything was taking. After calming herself down and talking it over with Tommy, we decided to practice small chunks of the Mass at home so that the kids could learn the responses. Karen conceded that the kids could be afforded some wiggle room, but we wanted them to know that they had to be the most reverent during the consecration. So we decided to start there.

We began a nightly habit of rehearsing the responses at the opening of the Liturgy of the Eucharist before bed. After a week of practice, it was go time for our kids on Sunday morning. And guess what? They got it! Instead of standing there with blank, disinterested looks as the rest of the congregation said, "It is right and just," *they actually joined in.* Of course, the chance of that happening at each Mass was completely dependent on their mood/thirst/hunger/mindfulness, but . . . baby steps!

One of the beautiful things about our Catholic faith is the consistency of the liturgy. Every Sunday, no matter if you're at your home parish or away on a vacation and visiting a parish, the liturgy is consistent. And though some adults complain that the consistency leads to boredom, the repetitive nature of the Mass is exactly what kids need. It gives them an opportunity to feel comfortable, slowly learn what to expect next, and have some idea of the time between the present moment and those post-liturgy donuts in the parish hall.

Teaching children the order of the Mass—the who, what, when, where, and why of our liturgy—is a great way to get them involved and instill a deep love for and understanding of it, which will (we hope) stick with them, even when they head off into the wild jungle of college.

Reading the Readings before Mass

We go to Mass with three relatively well-behaved children. Don't get us wrong, but their mere presence used to leave us feeling as if we had no idea what was going on during the Liturgy of the Word. You could have approached us immediately after Mass on any given Sunday, asked us to name any of the readings, and received a blank stare in reply. This was largely due to the fact that we were (and are) so concerned about how our children's behavior might impact our neighbors in nearby pews that, even when the kids were engaged and quietly attentive, we were still half focused on every noise coming from their direction.

So we decided to adopt the practice of reading the readings for Mass before we ever step foot in the church. After we agreed on this approach, Karen set the alarm on her phone for 8 a.m. Sunday as a reminder—and we didn't do it. Week after week, when the alarm went off, we would share a maybe-next-week look. Either the kids had slept in, or they woke up grumpy, or breakfast wasn't ready; for whatever reason, it didn't seem possible.

Then one week, while everyone was around the breakfast table, Tommy got out his phone, googled "today's readings," and pulled up the readings on the USCCB website. The Holy Spirit sure does work in mysterious ways, because the first reading for that Sunday was the always gripping story of Abraham and the sacrifice of Isaac (Genesis 22:1-14). As we read the story, we took several pauses, asked the kids questions about what we were reading, and asked them to make connections to the

Mass and to the trials Jesus faced. *And do you know what??!!* We had a really great conversation, and the kids were excited (we were too) that they understood what the story was about. The fact that we had a great experience the first time gave us the confidence to keep doing this, and the motivation to continue even when the readings are a bit over our heads.

We usually can't answer our kids' questions about the readings during Mass. So discussing the readings beforehand allows us to pause during an Old Testament story to ask why they think someone acted a certain way, or what they think St. Paul meant when he presented something in one of his letters. Most important, though, prereading gives us the opportunity to get their honest and childlike thoughts in relation to the message of Jesus in that day's Gospel. We're able to help guide their understanding of the readings and increase our own understanding. We're also able to bask in their amazing grasp of what is actually happening in sacred Scripture (this came as a surprise to us) and to get an inside look into the meaning of childlike faith.

Put Those Loud Voices to Work: Sing!

Our kids are always walking around the house singing the latest song from school at the top of their lungs—from "Slippery Fish" to their elementary school anthem, "Sunset School is number one! Teachers, students all have fun!" to repeating the same two lines from that *Moana* song. Why not put those loud voices and love of a catchy tune to good use and direct them toward making joyful sounds to the Lord?

Start with the hymns we sing at Mass. These memorable hymns—we've been singing them since we were children—still bring joy to our hearts. Encourage your kids to sing aloud at Mass and to fall in love with their own favorites along the way. Help them learn the hymns by listening to sacred music at home. Why not replace the streaming Taylor Swift in your kitchen as you make dinner with a few tracks from the Daughters of St. Paul?

By immersing our children in the music of our faith, we help them not only to enjoy it but also to praise God by singing wholeheartedly at Mass. And if singing is praying twice, a kid belting out the Salve Regina in the loudest voice possible has to be praying eleven or twelve times. From their lips to God's ears.

No Open Seating

When you have multiple kids to wrangle into submission through an hour-long Mass, thinking ahead of time about seating order is a must. You can't have the top two troublemakers next to each other, and you can't leave your loudest and most easily distracted kid more than an arm's length away from a parent. Planning ahead about who sits next to whom can be a lifesaver.

Flexibility is also key. Like the quarterback of an elite NFL team, parents have to be willing to make changes on the fly. You can't predict how your kids are going to behave on any given Sunday. The one who typically reads along and sings all the songs may have a bee in his bonnet one day, and you'll need to call an audible at the last moment. The three-year-old who hasn't been willing to go down for a nap in months might fall asleep despite a rousing and inspiring homily, at which point you'll need to clear space on the pew and make a little pillow with your purse.

When you're a family at Mass, you never know what's going to happen, and you have to be comfortable with the unknowns.

Consider Sitting Where You Can See

Shortly after James was born, we arrived at Mass and went where we thought we were assigned to go from then on: the cry room. Things weren't great. While the cry room works for some families, for ours it was like viewing Mass through a tiny window from the abyss of hell. Maybe that's overstating it, but let's just say it didn't work well for us. We persevered though, assuming the cry room was our best option.

After Mass one Sunday, when James was a little bit older, someone gave us a piece of advice: "Sit where your kids can see the action. Sit in the front pew." We pretty much laughed it off as crazy advice only a lunatic would follow, but after a few more failed attempts in the cry room, we decided to give it a shot. We sat up front, as a family, and braced ourselves for the worst while begging for Mary's intercession for the best.

Something about sitting up front worked for us. We're not sure if it was the priest staring our child into submission, the sight of Jesus on the crucifix right there in plain view, or the fact that James could see what was happening rather than staring at the back of someone's head for an hour, *but it worked*.

Now, one important thing to remember as a Catholic parent is that the things that work for some families can be disastrous for other families. No one should feel compelled to do something that doesn't work with their children, but for us sitting up front was revolutionary. We are reminded of this every time we show up for Mass and the front pews are already taken. We head to the back, and it's like the circus has rolled into town all over again.

For us, it's front pew or bust!

Whispering What's Going On

Even when you have a front-pew view and have followed all the advice we've given so far—prereading the readings, practicing responses at home, making expectations about singing and kneeling clear—children can still be puzzled by what's happening up there. We take everything for granted since we've been to thousands of Masses over the years, but kids can benefit from some brief (and quiet) explanations as the Mass unfolds. A quick and simple "This is where the bread becomes the actual Body of Christ" helps kids know why the bells are ringing at the moment of the elevation. Whispering, "Get ready to say, 'Lord, hear our prayer'" helps kids stay focused on the prayer of the faithful. Softly reminding, "The Gospel we're about to hear is the story about Jesus' life that we read before church" helps kids put everything in context.

Yes, Mass is a place for reverent silence (when possible). Yes, there is time to dissect the Mass on the ride home. However, teaching and instructing kids in the moment, when possible, has its benefits, especially because kids live so much in the present moment. The questions they have during the Sanctus are typically gone by the time they have a donut in hand, and it's often better to whisper an answer even during the most important part of the Mass than to let the question slip by, never to be asked again.

FOUR

LASAGNA IN THE HIGHEST!

Praying as a family

Karen's dad was one of twelve kids. Supper time at his childhood home on the farm was like a competition to see who could finish fastest and get seconds. Enjoying the meal and the company around you was not the point. So, being somewhere in the middle of the pack, he learned to eat quickly in order to get his fill.

Karen's mom was one of two kids. She grew up in a stricter household, with a more refined approach to mealtime. The first time Karen's dad went to dinner at his soon-to-be in-law's house, he sat down at the table and joined in the typical prayer most Catholic families squeeze in before chowing down: "Bless us, O Lord, and these, thy gifts, which we are about to receive from thy bounty. Through Christ, our Lord. Amen."

As soon as he said, "Amen," Dad picked up his fork and started digging in. The story goes that he looked up, halfway through his mashed potatoes, and realized they were still praying! "And may the souls of all the faithful departed, through the mercy of God, rest in peace. Amen."

It was an honest mistake, one most of us would have made, and thankfully Dad was still able to marry that woman in spite of his gaffe. That being said, Karen's parents continued adding the prayer for the departed to the end of their prayer before dinner, and we have carried that tradition into our family. Tommy has especially enjoyed watching our guests pick up their forks only to lay them back down once they realize we're still going.

It's been wonderful to watch our children learn to pray this prayer, especially to hear the charming ways they slip up from time to time. When Paul was little, he routinely closed out his dinner prayer with this fun version: "May the souls in the faithful *apartment*, through the mercy of God, rest in peace. Amen."

Children and adults alike are prone to "mistakes" while praying, but that shouldn't stop us.

Why Pray Together?

When it comes to prayer as a family—even something as simple as grace before meals—everyone is well aware that it's important, but most of us are wondering how in the world we're supposed to do it. Stories of families who pray a nightly Rosary with their toddlers confound us. We can barely make it through the first three Hail Marys, and yet we hear rumors of other families who pray all twenty mysteries before bed each night, with their three-year-old praying the Our Father in Latin and then naming all the popes in order, from St. Peter to Pope Francis. That doesn't work for us. However, we do have some simple ideas that have helped us establish a habit of family prayer in the midst of a busy and often overwhelming life.

When things are running smoothly, it's easy to incorporate prayer into family life, but when the going gets tough, the inevitable question "Is this even worth it?" will rear its ugly head. When we first tried to pray as a family before putting the kids to bed, we found it easy to skip prayers on days when the kids needed an early bedtime to help Mommy and Daddy avoid a nervous breakdown. One night, in the midst of a bedtime routine that had no time for books or two full minutes of brushing teeth, we tucked the kids in, kissed them good night, and tried to hurry out the door. James popped a question that stopped us dead in our tracks: "Aren't we going to say our prayers?"

In our parenting panic to get the kids to sleep as quickly as possible, we made the unconscious decision to skip our nightly prayer routine, *and he noticed*. We realized, in that moment, that we owed it to our kids and ourselves to slow down, say a prayer, and keep that time as time set aside to reach out to God, even when we feel rushed. Over the previous few years, we had impressed on our children the utmost importance of prayer, and James incorporated that into his worldview. When he saw us contradict what we had taught him, he pointed that out. That moment showed us two things: first, that our dedication to prayer was paying off for our children and, second, that having a designated time for prayer would help to keep us on track—and if it didn't, our eight-year-old was right there, ready to remind us.

Teaching Prayers Step-by-Step

As we stood in the back of St. Francis parish in San Jose, attending Mass while visiting Karen's parents, Tommy whispered the Nicene Creed into then-three-month-old James' ear. Sure, he was a bit young to know what the creed was all about, but it felt right to start teaching him our Catholic prayers even though he hadn't started babbling yet. As we've gone through the process of teaching prayers to each of our children, we've come to see that kids are never too young to start hearing, absorbing, and ultimately learning the prayers.

When it comes to fostering prayer in the family, you'll find that there are many things you want to do, but you can't do them all at once unless you want to drive yourself crazy. So where are you supposed to start?

First, you have to be patient and let your kids go at their own pace. Not everyone is going to be blessed with a four-year-old who walks around praying the psalms from memory. In reality, we're more likely to be blessed with a kid proudly scream-singing "Lasagna in the highest," much to our embarrassment, at Mass. Be patient with them, and don't let yourself be overwhelmed by stress or arbitrary deadlines for when they have to know their prayers.

Second, start with the basics. Our faith has a wealth of beautiful, deep, and lengthy prayers that can help us grow closer to

Jesus and find that inner peace we're all looking for. Kids can learn those when they're ready. For now, focus on the Sign of the Cross, Our Father, Hail Mary, and Glory Be. These simple prayers are powerful despite (or maybe because of) their simplicity, and kids can typically learn them at an early age.

When our kids are around the age of two, we do a little back-and-forth with them, letting them finish each line of a prayer as we go along. Having heard the Hail Mary over and over, for example, they start to pick up the last word of each sentence:

Us: *Hail Mary, full of*
Them: *Grace!*
Us: *The Lord is with*
Them: *Thee!*

Initially, they only know a few words of each prayer, but this little exercise starts them on the path of memorizing prayers that will strengthen and comfort them later in their lives. For now, it's a fun way to share the prayer, let them grow into it, and catch some cute mistakes or serious emoting along the way. There are few things Tommy enjoys more than hearing our three-year-old Andrew say, with gusto, the last word of each part of the prayer to St. Michael. Sure, he may not know it all by heart quite yet, but after hearing it every single week after Mass, he's learned enough of it to make us proud.

Of course, not every kid is going to be ready to say nine words of the Hail Mary at the age of two, and many may not be ready to make the Sign of the Cross before kindergarten.

That's okay. Seriously, that's okay. Let them move at their own pace. As long as you lead by example, they will eventually learn, even if the effort doesn't come as naturally as you might have hoped.

ROFP (Rolling on the Floor Praying)

As we sat around the kids' bedroom and delved into our bedtime prayers one night, our six-year-old joined in but in his own unique way. As we prayed to our guardian angels to be there to light, guard, rule, and guide, he rolled around on the floor, tossing a pillow up in the air over and over again. Tommy tugged on his shirt and gave him the "get up" stare, and he promptly complied.

Days later, during the same nighttime prayer, Tommy was lying on one of the kids' beds while praying. Of course, the kids promptly called him out for the same posture he had a problem with earlier in the week. Talking it over later, we came up with a couple of guidelines that we've carried with us from prayer experience to prayer experience.

First, we've set explicit boundaries around important elements of family prayer time. It isn't fair for us to expect the kids to sit or kneel if we don't make that clear ahead of time. Communication is key to successful family prayer. So our kids now know the length of time we're going to pray and what we expect in terms of their behavior and posture during prayer.

Second, we have to mirror those expectations. We can tell our kids until we're blue in the face to kneel or sit with their hands peacefully folded, but if we cruise through prayers lying on a bed as Tommy did, they're not going to listen. Think about your expectations and what will work for your family, and then communicate and model those expectations.

Correcting Mistakes and Using Common Sense

As we mentioned earlier, kids are bound to make mistakes when they're first learning how to pray. And though slipups like "souls in the faithful apartment" may be sweet, we have a duty as parents to provide correction. But we must always do so with gentleness.

Scripture often speaks of the need for a gentle, kind spirit when we approach others. St. Peter tells us, in his first letter, that when explaining the faith to someone who wants to know the reason for our hope, we should speak "with gentleness and reverence" (3:16). St. Paul tells us, in his Second Letter to Timothy, to correct opponents "with kindness" (2:25). Kids are usually trying their best to say what they think the prayer says, and an abrasive correction to their slipups could lead to a pretty negative reaction to prayer in general. (And if your children are even one-tenth as sensitive as ours, it will probably also lead to tears.) After all, even we adults make prayer-related mistakes from time to time, and we prefer to have someone correct us gently and encourage us to continue on.

Taking a commonsense approach to practical matters can also help get your kids on board with prayer. If you want them to focus on your prayer of blessing before dinner, for example, don't put the food on their plates until you've wrapped up the prayers. We've taken this approach, and it's helped prayers go more smoothly. It would be hard to blame our little three-year-old for digging into Karen's scratch mac and cheese before the final Sign of the Cross if it's smelling absolutely perfect right under his nose. (In full disclosure, last night we watched that three-year-old devour a slice of pizza while we were still praying. Oh well, baby steps.)

"I Can't Think of Anything I'm Thankful For"

Part of our bedtime prayer routine is to thank God for the blessings we have received throughout the day. We're pretty good at letting the kids fling the door wide open on their options, and we've heard everything from "Thank you, God, for our chickens" to "Thank you for Andrew not punching me today." But one evening, our son Paul declared, "I can't think of anything I'm thankful for."

Tommy, being the impatient and easily frustrated parent that he is, went off a bit. He described loads of things Paul could thank God for and drove home the point by telling him there are kids in *our very own city* who don't have a place to lay their heads down at night, don't have any toys, don't get seconds and thirds and fourths at dinner, and on and on and on.

After the tirade, Paul looked thoughtful but came to the same conclusion: "I *still* can't think of anything that I'm thankful for." As Tommy turned into a boiling teakettle about to overflow, Karen took a different approach. She gently guided Paul to the next part of our usual bedtime prayers, allowing him to omit the "counting his blessings" part, and everything went along peacefully.

Tommy was committing one of the big errors associated with teaching children how to pray: proceeding as though prayer is something to be checked off a religious to-do list rather than a means of fostering a love for God and a relationship with him. All of us are going to come up against times when our children simply don't want to pray. After all, *we* go through times like that, right? And for some reason, we feel that it's all right for us to feel that way but not for our kids. We have to make our kids keep praying even when they don't feel like it. This comes from our focus on that to-do list mentality and our fear that if our kids don't pray all the time, even when they don't want to, they're not going to pray as adults.

But our goal here is to help our kids form a true love of prayer, to see it as necessary in their lives and as critical to developing their relationship with God. With that in mind, it's clear that "forcing" them to pray or saying, "Too bad, you *have* to," may not be the best method to help them fall in love with praying. A gentle, thoughtful approach can be tricky to put into practice, but it's really the best way to ensure that kids see prayer not as a punishment of sorts but, rather, as something they can return to freely when they feel ready, something that can develop and grow inside them. They still have to stay with the family as we pray and remain respectful during prayer time, so they don't get off the hook completely.

It's worth reiterating that a powerful witness of prayer in our own lives is key to helping our children develop that appreciation of prayer in their lives. Archbishop Charles Chaput of Philadelphia may have put that idea best when he said,

> [I]f parents love God, children see and learn faith. Parents who pray together teach by the way they live that God is real; that he is present, listening, and eager to be part of our lives. . . . A life of prayer makes us fully human because it makes us real; it brings us out of ourselves, again and again, into conversation with the Author of life Himself—the God who made and loves us, and created everything we know.[5]

Creating a Sacred Space

Scrolling through Instagram one May afternoon while he should have been working, Tommy noticed a lot of Catholics posting photos of their home altars. Beautiful yet simple, these little areas within their homes were inspiring. Some were adorned with crucifixes, some with statues of Mary, and some even had relics. The idea of having a space within one's home that felt set apart, like church, spoke to Tommy as he scrolled through his feed.

A few years later, we finally decided to go for it and set up our own modest home altar. It isn't much, but it does feel different from the rest of the house. There's something peaceful and encouraging about a place within the home that's dedicated to the Lord and to prayer.

In the document *Lumen Gentium* from the Second Vatican Council, we read, "The family is, so to speak, the domestic church."[6] With that in mind, the United States Conference of Catholic Bishops has a list of great ideas for making the home a sacred space. (We list three of them here; the rest of the list can be found at the bishops' website, usccb.org/beliefs-and-teach/vocations/parents/tools-for-building-a-domestic-church.cfm.)

- Have a crucifix in a prominent place in the home and in every bedroom.
- Welcome into your home and support priests, brothers, sisters, deacons, and lay ministers in the Church.
- Allow your children to witness you in private prayer. Encourage your children to pray daily on their own, to listen for God's call, and, if heard, to respond.

Crucifixes throughout the home keep the entire family focused on God and his role in our lives. Not only can we look up and remember his protection as we go about our day, but we can also look to the crucifix during times of pain and sorrow. We can see what Jesus went through and try to imitate his example of how to suffer well.

We talked about inviting priests and other religious over in the last chapter; it's another great way to make your home a sacred space. Tommy finds it pretty intimidating to invite a priest over, perhaps even more intimidating than when he first asked Karen out on a date. (Okay, fine, Karen asked Tommy out on a date first; but that just goes to show how intimidated he was.)

Inviting priests over reminds our children of the fact that we're part of a community of Catholics, helps them see that priests are normal people, like us, and makes our homes feel more sacred.

Allowing children to witness you in private prayer may feel a bit awkward, but showing them, rather than merely telling them, how prayer unfolds is a powerful teaching tool. Remember the impact on young Karol Wojtyla when he saw his father praying in the middle of the night. If we allow ourselves to be vulnerable by opening up our private prayer life to our children, we show them that a sacred space can be found anytime we decide to call out to the Lord.

Rookie Prayer Families, Unite!

If you are new to praying as a family, it can feel weird or awkward at first, and that's fine. Prayer isn't like a switch that a family can flip and suddenly the kids are walking into the kitchen every day at 3 p.m. to remind their parents that it's time to pray the Divine Mercy Chaplet. A good prayer life, especially as a family unit, takes time. It's a step-by-step journey, filled with trial and error.

Anyone who has busted out the rosary beads with three kids ages eight and under will tell you it's not going to work right out of the gate. Only through practice will a family settle into a specific devotion that's a good fit for them. And making sure it's a good fit is something to keep your eye on. All of us, as individuals and as families, will figure out that certain prayer styles and devotions click with us, while others do not.

We have to listen to that tiny voice inside that says, "Maybe this isn't the best; let's try something different," and be willing to go with it and seek out another way of praying together. It's okay to do a complete 180, leave a devotion behind, and try something else. You can also try praying as a family at a different time of the day rather than before bed, when your kids are tired. Look for any options that make it easier, more comfortable, and more possible for your family to pray together.

Part of the problem for many families, including ours, is that we try to squeeze ourselves into a particular way of praying rather than considering first what might work for our family. Just because Mary and Joseph down the street are able to pray the Liturgy of the Hours with their kids doesn't mean that's going to be the family prayer style that works for us. So let's take a look at some examples of prayers that can be used within a family and see what sticks.

Start Slow, Start Small

If you haven't incorporated prayer into the busyness of daily life and you're beginning from square one, it can help to start small. Even though you may want to make a big push toward a solid prayer life for your family, you'll have more success if you ease into things. After all, holiness is achieved in small steps, not one giant leap to the finish line. Take it slow.

Starting with a prayer before dinner is a great way to get going. Pegged to dinner, it's easy to remember to do. It forces everyone to pause and think about God before jumping in and devouring their meatballs on spaghetti night, *and* it fosters thankfulness in a world where the importance of counting one's blessings is easily and often overlooked.

Keeping it simple and sweet can break the ice and start your family down the path of recognizing the value of prayer and, specifically, the value of praying together as a family.

The Rosary

This is a Catholic book, so we have to include *the* Catholic prayer, right? The Rosary is a beautiful prayer that seems designed for a family-style experience. Plenty of prayers to switch off among the older kids, beads to keep the little ones occupied, and even meditations on the Gospel to ensure that family members are getting their daily dose of Scripture. (Unfortunately, the beads are also pretty good weapons, and at our house, it doesn't take long for our three sons to start spinning them, instigating an all-out brawl.)

When introducing the Rosary into family prayer, it's okay to do so in small steps. Heed the words of St. Thérèse of Lisieux: "Do small things with great love." God doesn't ask us to go through all twenty mysteries of the Rosary—or even one mystery—every night, with all our kids maintaining perfect attention, discipline, and focus. Rather, like a good parent, he asks us to do something small but to do it with great love in our hearts.

We can ease into the Rosary by simply saying an Our Father and three Hail Marys and then closing it out. We can progress to doing one of the mysteries set aside for the day (instead of all five). We can simply say each of the prayers associated with the Rosary once, to help our kids become familiar with them.

We also have to be willing to step back and decide if the Rosary is right for our families. Not every Catholic family is going to have a charism for praying the Rosary together. We know that's not a popular take, but it's true. As Catholics we can fall into the trap of feeling as if *we have to* pray the Rosary, but the Church has many prayers and spiritualities that might work better for us as a family. With a little introspection and working from trial and error, you can determine which prayers and spiritual styles resonate with your kids.

Reading Scripture as a Family

We often, but not always, incorporate Bible stories into our night-time routine. Currently here's what works for our young family.

Our kids each get to pick a book for us to read to them before bedtime prayers and hit-the-sack time. While they typically go for the popular kids' books overflowing from their shelf, sometimes we gently encourage them to go for a story from the Bible. We've cracked open various children's Bibles and jumped right into the pithy versions of stories from the days of Adam and Eve, Moses, and most important, Jesus. The more we discuss Scripture with our kids, as we do with the readings before Sunday Mass, and the more we read Bible stories with them, the more familiar and connected they become with the faith.

For every *Go, Dog, Go*, there should be an Adam and Eve. For every *Elephant and Piggie*, there should be a nativity story. And yes, for every *Harry Potter*, there should be a multiplication of the loaves and fishes. Bible stories help children see God's faithfulness and his action in history. Delving into his word through these stories helps lay the groundwork for understanding what our faith is truly all about.

Thank You, Please, I'm Sorry, and I Love You

The four most important things that we can say in *any* relationship are thank you, please, I'm sorry, and I love you. These four statements should be part of daily life in our family and also part of our prayer life, to help us grow in our relationship with God.

We have used these four statements to help our children establish a nice structure for prayer—to see prayer as conversational and spontaneous as they grow in a relationship with God. They can use these points—and we can use them in family prayer time—to count their blessings, ask for forgiveness for times they fell short, request divine help for upcoming endeavors, and affirm love for God and one another.

Helping our kids become comfortable with conversing with God when they are young can open them up to the fact that faith is about a relationship, and no relationship can improve or succeed for any length of time without an open and honest back-and-forth dialogue. *Thank you, please, I'm sorry,* and *I love you* are great ways to put kids at ease and get their minds flowing into a conversation with God, where their relationship with him can flourish.

Pope Francis' Five Fingers

Andrew's godparents introduced us to Pope Francis' idea of praying with our five fingers. It quickly became one of the kids' favorite ways to pray together.

We start this prayer with our thumb, the finger that is closest to us. Our thumb reminds us to start our prayer by praying for those who are closest to us: our families, our friends, our coworkers, our neighbors. The index finger reminds us to pray for those who teach us, instruct us, and heal us. Our teachers at school and at religious education classes, our doctors, priests, and bishops—we should pray for them when we come together to pray as a family. Our tallest finger is next, and it reminds us to pray for our leaders and those in positions of authority. In our current culture, where those in leadership positions are subject to constant mocking, negativity, and gossip, it's especially important to pray for our leaders.

Our ring finger comes next, and Pope Francis points out that this is actually our weakest finger. The ring finger reminds us to pray for the least among us: the sick, the poor, those facing problem after problem after problem in their lives. We will be judged according to how we cared for the weakest, and praying for them daily is one important element of that care.

Finally, we move to the pinky, the smallest of our fingers. The pinky reminds us to pray for ourselves. Once we have offered up prayers on the other four fingers, we are able to see ourselves and our needs in the correct perspective. We ought to pray for ourselves because we need God's help in order to grow in holiness as individuals and as a family.

Pope Francis' five-finger prayer is a great way to help children remember who to pray for simply by looking at their hands.

Short and Sweet

Kids love things that are short and sweet, so lastly, we want to encourage the value of a quick prayer they can pull out whenever they need it. The extremely simple and extremely powerful "Jesus, I trust in you," from the Divine Mercy image given to St. Faustina, is one that comes to mind. Whenever there's trouble brewing—be it with homework, a difficult interaction with a peer, or an anxiety-provoking class presentation—kids can remind themselves that Jesus is in control. This helps bring calm to an otherwise tense situation. It works for us adults too.

Being able to get your kids into praying throughout the day is a huge key toward keeping them close to the faith and encouraging their relationship with Jesus. If they learn the power of prayer as kids, it'll carry them through what life will deal out the rest of their lives.

FIVE

ALL YOU HOLY MEN AND WOMEN

Incorporating the lives of the saints into the life of your family

When we were expecting our second child, we *knew* we were having a girl. Our sister-in-law was also pregnant and due a few months before us. There were several boys in our family already, and we felt certain one of us was bound to have a girl. Then, when our sister-in-law found out they were having a boy, we became even more sure that *our* baby *had* to be a girl.

We had a list a mile long of girl names we liked. Several of our friends commented that it was a "girl year" because everyone they knew was having a girl, so ours was probably a girl too. Plus, Karen was carrying wide. And the trick where you put your wedding ring on a necklace and swing it over your belly? It went in a circle, another sure sign of a girl. It was all adding up to the fact that we were definitely having a girl. We had a list a mile long of girl names we liked.

If you read our bio, you know what happened. In spite of all the evidence assuring us that a daughter was in our future, we found out that the baby was a boy—the seventh boy among Tommy's siblings' kids.

The debate on what to name our son went 'round and 'round for a while. It seems silly to us now, but we were not prepared for picking another boy's name. Choosing a name that wasn't a repeat in our family or too close phonetically was a bit of a challenge.

That's when Karen's mom pulled out her calendar. "When's the due date again?" she asked. "June 8," Karen replied. Her mom began to throw out some suggestions. "Well, if he's a little early, there's St. Justin, St. Peter, and St. Charles on the first, second, and third of June. June 13 is the feast of St. Anthony, my favorite saint! June 13 would be great!"

She excitedly continued, "St. Boniface, St. Norbert, and St. Ephrem the next week. And if he waits a while, St. Romuald or St. Aloysius. But don't let him wait that long, okay?" In the end, our sweet Paul came bright and early on June 13, and much to the surprise (and annoyance) of Karen's mom, we did not end up naming him according to the feast day. While her suggestions didn't make the baby-naming cut, they certainly reminded us that our Catholic calendar is brimming with days to celebrate and great saints to honor.

Getting to know the saints and honoring them are excellent ways to help your kids see what it means to love the Lord and live a virtuous life. Not boring!

Find Your Family's Saints

A simple way to begin celebrating the lives of saints is to choose saints who are connected to your family in some way. Celebrate their feasts specifically. Not only will starting this way give you a chance to catch your breath as the liturgical calendar keeps chugging forward—even though you have soccer practice on Thursday *and* Saturday—but also, starting with saints who resonate with your family can add deeper meaning to your celebration. Take time, as a family, to explore exactly why you feel close to a saint.

For example, you can honor and remember the saints who share your name, the names of your children, and the names of other important family members. While we're still on the lookout for St. Karen, and Tommy is still coming to terms with the fact that his namesake is best known for his profound doubt, we routinely recall St. James, St. Paul, St. Andrew, and St. Luke as we go through the year, making sure to mark their feasts, even if only in small ways.

If your children aren't named after saints who pop up on the liturgical calendar, that's okay! Take a look at different patronages and see which saints connect with your family. There are saints designated as patrons for just about every profession, artistic endeavor, social outreach, nation, illness, and need out there. There are sure to be a few that speak to your heart and the hearts of your children.

Get close to these saints, learn everything you can about them, and foster a relationship with them through prayer. Make sure to tell their stories to your kids.

So How Many Saints Are There, Anyway?

It's well-known that Catholics honor the holy heroes who have gone before us, and we ask them to pray for us. Sometimes we joke that it's definitely a feast day even if you don't know it yet. So how many saints are there?

No one really knows, because the official saint-making process didn't start until the tenth century or so. Prior to that, naming a deceased person a saint happened more informally, by general agreement. But saint making did begin right from the start, in the earliest days of the Church. The very first Christians named saints, starting with the martyrs.

Now, thanks to the Internet, we have instant access to information about many of the approximately ten thousand people honored as saints. That's right, we said ten thousand. That calendar can get crowded!

Take October 4 as an example. Many Catholics recognize this as the feast of St. Francis of Assisi, one of the most popular saints in the history of the Church. And yet he's not the only one who lays claim to the fourth day of the tenth month. Francis shares his day with lesser-known saints like St. Adauctus, St. Ammon, St. Aurea, Sts. Crispus and Gaius, St. Domnina, St. Hierotheus, St. Mark (not *that* St. Mark), St. Peter of Damascus, St. Petronius, *and* St. Quintius. Yes, the Church celebrates twelve saints on October 4.

How about December 12, well-known around the Catholic world as the feast of Our Lady of Guadalupe (as well as Karen's birthday, for those wanting to send presents)? Mary shares this day with fine folks like St. Abra, St. Agatha of Wimborne, St. Alexander, St. Ammonaria, St. Colman of Glendalough, St. Columba of Terryglass, St. Corentin, St. Corentius, St. Edburga, St. Finian of Clonard—and several others, but we think you get the picture.

The point we want to drive home is just how many saints we have watching out for us, praying for us, and helping us get by every single day, whether we realize it or not and whether we've heard of them or not.

Traditional and Not So Traditional

You may have noticed, when we tossed out those lists of saints for October 4 and December 12, that although there are plenty of canonized saints we know pretty well, there are lots more we've never heard of. You can stick to Francis, Mary, Joseph, and the usual crew when trying to think of saints who match up well with your family, but you don't have to. Why not go for a Ceolwulf, Frodobert, or Gamo?

It's fun to choose and grow close to a saint most people haven't heard of—and there are many of them! Their stories of heroic virtue are out there, waiting to be read and shared with our children. These men and women can inspire and accompany us on the path of growing in virtue.

You might introduce your family to St. Rose Philippine Duchesne, who opened the first free school west of the Missouri River; St. Nonna, who was the matriarch of one of the holiest families this side of Nazareth; or St. Genevieve, who led prayers that stopped Attila the Hun in his tracks and kept

Paris safe. Be brave! Jump into the ocean that is the communion of saints, and embrace some of our lesser-known sisters and brothers there.

Celebrating with Class

If you'd like to celebrate some feast days with cool traditions but don't know where to start, never fear. We're happy to present solid ideas to help you get on the path toward living the liturgical calendar.

—ST. MICHAEL—
September 29

Also known as Michaelmas, the feast of St. Michael has its roots in the Middle Ages, when it was celebrated as a holy day of obligation. St. Michael, the greatest of all the archangels, is best known for defeating Satan and his minions in the war in heaven (see the Book of Revelation, chapter 12).

Get busy in the kitchen preparing the traditional Michaelmas foods, like goose, sweet bread, carrots, and blackberries. Share the powerful Prayer to St. Michael with your children. Decorate your home with beautiful daisies in honor of the archangel, reciting this rhyme:

> The Michaelmas daisies, among dead weeds,
> Bloom for St Michael's valorous deeds.

St. Michael kicked Satan's backside, so he deserves quite the celebration.

—ST. BRIGID—
February 1

This patron saint of Ireland, who lived between 451 and 525, is known for giving her family's entire store of butter to the poor, only to have the stock replenished after offering up a prayer. She was a religious sister, an abbess, and the founder of several monasteries of nuns in Kildare. Numerous miracles have been attributed to her.

This *other* patron of Ireland (you all know St. Patrick, right?) has a bunch of customs associated with her feast day—a day that is traditionally celebrated at the midway point between winter and spring. Kids will enjoy making a St. Brigid cross, a symbol of Ireland, from pipe cleaners or raffia (you can find instructions online). Or consider leaving oats and butter on the windowsill for her and corn on the cob for her cow—the cow that helped keep St. Brigid alive as a baby, when her mother was unable to nurse her.

You might also tie a ribbon on a tree, an ancient Irish custom symbolizing the legend of Brigid's seemingly endlessly expanding cloak spread over the land to mark the place where she would build her monastery. It was said that St. Brigid blessed these ribbons as she traveled through the land, endowing them with healing power.

These and many other customs can help your family celebrate one of Ireland's great saints. And once the kids go to bed, there's nothing wrong with a little Guinness, Bailey's, or Irish coffee to cap off a great occasion.

—ST. NICHOLAS—
December 6

You might or might not talk about Santa Claus with your children, telling tales of jolly old St. Nick and his voyage around the world to deliver presents to good boys and girls. (See chapter 7 for the debate on this topic.) But do you celebrate the actual St. Nick?

St. Nicholas was a bishop in Asia Minor, and while he may not have traveled the world with a sack full of toys, his penchant for gift giving does have some connection to the Santa Claus myth. According to one story, St. Nicholas helped a poor man pay the dowries that would enable his three daughters to get married. Under cover of night, St. Nick tossed three purses filled with gold coins into the home of this family, covering the amount of the required dowries. Other versions of the tale speak of Nicholas throwing the money down the chimney, as a sign that the gift came from God, or tossing the purses through the window, only to have them land in the daughters' stockings, which were hanging over the fire to dry. Sound familiar?

Nowadays families around the world celebrate the feast of St. Nicholas by placing gold coins, small toys, or gold-wrapped candy coins in the shoes of children as they are sleeping.

—ST. FRANCIS OF ASSISI—
October 4

St. Francis of Assisi, one of the Church's most well-known and beloved saints, was from a family of prosperous silk merchants. He left everything behind to devote himself to Our Lord in holy poverty. There are many engaging children's books about him that make it easy to share his life story with kids.

Francis' feast is a special day when man's best friend gets to come to church with the family! The blessing of pets (typically in the church parking lot, for obvious reasons) is a tradition that incorporates St. Francis' love of nature and animals into the beauty of our Catholic faith. We haven't managed to get our hens to church yet, but we're working out the details for next year.

If you aren't able to make it to church on October 4, you might want to treat your pets at home in honor of their patron. Don't forget to make a treat for the family too; an Italian dessert, such as tiramisu or cannoli, sounds about right.

—ST. BARBARA—
December 4

According to tradition, Barbara was a mid-third-century martyr, the daughter of a rich pagan who locked her up in a tower in order to protect her from the world. As she gazed on the earth from high up in the tower, she was drawn to the beauty of creation and, more specifically, to the Creator. She became a Christian and for this was condemned to death.

Barbara's father carried out the death sentence and, according to the legend, was struck by lightning in punishment. This led to St. Barbara being named the patron of armorers, military engineers, gunsmiths, tunnelers, miners, and anyone else who works with cannons and explosives.

The peaceful way to celebrate St. Barbara's feast is to cut small stems off soon-to-blossom trees and "force" them to bloom. (You can find detailed information online for forcing flowers to bloom.) Folklore has it that the person in the family who ends up with the most blooms on their branch by Christmas Eve is Mary's favorite! Talk about a tradition ripe for competition in a young, growing family.

The less peaceful way to celebrate the feast involves St. Barbara's patronage over explosives. You've guessed it! St. Barbara's feast day is quite possibly best celebrated by pulling out the fireworks (where legal, of course) and setting them off in honor of this holy hero. Make sure to save a few from the Fourth of July.

—ST. LUCY—
December 13

Here's another close-to-Christmas feast day, celebrated in a classic close-to-Christmas way.

St. Lucy was an early-fourth-century Sicilian martyr who, according to tradition, rejected a potential husband. He then denounced her as a Christian, which led to her martyrdom.

But before that, Lucy secretly visited and served Christians who lived in the catacombs during this time of persecution.

Because the catacombs were dark, she is often depicted carrying candles to light her way. An ancient custom tied to that candle-bearing—the wearing of a crown of greenery topped with lighted candles—is perfect for a family celebration, minus the lit candles. According to this custom, the oldest girl in the family wears the crown and brings the family sweet rolls in the early morning of the feast day.

The name *Lucy* means "light." Also, her feast is close to the winter solstice, with its trending toward spring—these facts and her visits to the catacombs explain the significance of the candles.

Now, unless you like to deal with fire hazards and the possibility of hot wax dripping on your child's face, we suggest an Advent-wreath-like decoration of felt or paper with fake candles that girls (or, in our case, Mom) wear as they bring treats to the family at breakfast. Accompany this great tradition with a brief prayer, and you have the makings of a fun family celebration in honor of this great saint.

—ST. JOSEPH THE WORKER—
May 1

The main man, St. Joseph, most definitely deserves our honor on his feast days. Yes, he has two, and we discuss them both in this book. (See chapter 6 for the solemnity of St. Joseph, March 19.) Because he is the foster father of Jesus and a favorite among Catholics, and because many of us name our children after him, we think it's right to give him double billing as a top saint our children need to know.

As the earthly father of Jesus and as a working man, Joseph's life is an example to all dads and husbands and to men and women of every vocation. Always listening to God, never questioning or complaining, St. Joseph knew what it meant to be a humble servant of Our Lord, and he pulled this off despite being the only imperfect member of a *very* Holy Family.

This is a good day to speak with your children about what it means to work hard in everything we are called to do. Talk with your kids about why we persevere in work, even if we're tired or bored or want to give up. What does it mean to work cheerfully? What does it mean to listen for God's direction as we work? How do they think St. Joseph felt about his work when he was tired or had to deal with a grumbling customer? This is a good day for everyone in the family to think about our attitude toward work as we serve others and go the extra mile.

Pope St. John Paul II wrote an apostolic exhortation about St. Joseph, *Redemptoris Custos,* and it makes good reading for the adults in the family. In the section on work, the pope reminds us,

> Work was the daily expression of love in the life of the Family of Nazareth. The Gospel specifies the kind of work Joseph did in order to support his family: he was a carpenter. This simple word sums up Joseph's entire life. . . .
>
> . . . "St. Joseph is the model of those humble ones that Christianity raises up to great destinies; . . . he is the proof that in order to be a good and genuine follower of Christ,

there is no need of great things—it is enough to have the common, simple and human virtues, but they need to be true and authentic."[7]

The Queen of All Saints

We couldn't pull together a list of saintly celebrations without mentioning the mother of all saints. Mary offers the perfect example of a Christian life well lived. She always said yes to the will of God, no matter how much it pierced her heart to do so.

Many feast days over the course of the year honor Mary. The entire month of May, for example, is dedicated to Our Lady. Many families celebrate by creating a May altar in her honor, decorated with pictures, candles, holy cards, and plenty of fresh flowers to remind us of her beauty and purity.

Similarly, we celebrate the Rosary during the month of October. In addition to taking up the beads more frequently during the month, we can also celebrate with a dinner-table-sized rosary with cupcakes standing in for the beads (not to be eaten by oneself, of course). We can also add one Marian prayer to our family prayers each week until we know them all by heart—the Memorare, the Hail Holy Queen, the Magnificat, and so on.

In addition to these month-long celebrations of Mary, we can celebrate the solemnity of the Holy Mother of God (January 1), the Annunciation (March 25, nine months before the birth of Jesus), the Visitation (May 31), the memorial of the Immaculate Heart (the Saturday after Corpus Christi), the solemnity of the Assumption (August 15), the Queenship of Mary (August 22), Mary's birthday (September 8), the memorial of Our Lady of Sorrows (September 15), Our Lady of the Rosary (October 7), the Presentation of Mary (November 21), the Immaculate Conception (December 8), and more. We can also celebrate Mary on the feast days of some of her apparitions: Our Lady of Lourdes on February 11, Our Lady of Fatima on May 13, and Our Lady of Guadalupe on December 12.

Well, our calendar is pretty full; how about yours?

Don't Forget Your Parish Saint

In case you feel you don't have enough days to celebrate, we've got one last possibility for you. Your family has an opportunity every year to celebrate the patron saint of your local parish. At our parish, St. Michael's, we have an annual festival in honor of our patron, as do many other parishes for their patron saint. But creating a small family celebration on your parish patron's special day can also help your family feel more connected to the parish community, more connected to the saint watching over that community, and more connected to the communion of saints as a whole. Invite other families to come over to celebrate with you (think potluck) as a way of fostering a sense of community, something that is too often lacking at the parish level.

Now let's turn to some ideas for bringing the saints into your family's day-to-day life independent of the calendar.

Reading about the Saints

Our kids are captivated by stories about St. Francis and the wolf, St. Kateri and her brave conversion, and St. Patrick spreading the faith throughout Ireland. The saints didn't set out on the adventures of their lives in order to obtain earthly treasure at their journey's end. They did everything for Jesus and his Church, and their lives are jam-packed with way more risk and courage than some fictional story about a wizard boy from England.

There are loads of children's Catholic books about the saints, and reading them as a family can keep the saints alive in your home. We enjoy reading the typical biographical stories, and our children also love the historical fiction of the *Chime Travelers* series by Lisa Hendey. Lisa's books focus on a present-day Catholic family with three young children, two of whom magically travel through time to meet and walk alongside various saints of the Church.

A nice feature of this series is that the families in the books are Catholic families who do actual Catholic things, which is not something you typically get out of a good bedtime story. They go to Confession, go to Mass, and help clean the church as a way of giving back to the community. Even though the books are fiction, they've helped us show our kids—in a fun, engaging way—families who are like ours in so many ways.

Chime Traveler books are full of details about the lives of the saints whom the time-traveling children encounter. Karen has gotten into the habit of reading one chapter per night to the kids on days when we have enough time after bedtime prayers. The kids can't wait to hear what's going to happen next.

Listening to the Lives of the Saints

Considering all you have to do just to make it through the day, it can be overwhelming to find time to share the faith with the kids. You want to talk about the saints, and you might even be doing some of the things we've been discussing in this chapter, but how can you do even more and still keep your head above water?

We've realized two things: 1) even though we work hard to refrain from overscheduling ourselves and our kids, we still feel busy to our limit; and 2) we spend a lot of time driving to various places in the minivan. All that time in the minivan (to school, faith formation, the store, church, Grandma and Grandpa's house, and so on) was being wasted. Sure, we actively tried to engage our kids in conversation, but it's difficult to carry on a conversation with kids in the back of a van who barely speak above a squeak (although they *do* seem to be able to raise the volume to whatever level they want, on their terms).

And then we found *Glory Stories* from Holy Heroes. *Glory Stories* is an audio collection of dramatized versions of the lives of the saints, professionally crafted and acted; some of the actors are little kids. Holy Heroes has produced *Glory Stories* for many favorite saints: St. Faustina, St. Maximilian Kolbe, St. Teresa of Calcutta, St. Rose of Lima, St. Joan of Arc, St. Anthony of

Padua, St. Juan Diego, and that's just naming the ones we have in our glove box at this moment.

Our kids are completely captivated by the stories, and they have learned a great deal about the lives of the saints in a way that really sticks with them. We listen to them over and over and over, and they're good enough for us adults to enjoy as well.

Having Saints around the House

When people look around your house, do they know you are a Catholic family? Tommy has often pondered this question as we move furniture around the living room, hang pictures in the hallway, or slap a new coat of paint on the walls. When people come to visit our home for the first time, what do they see that shows them what we believe and cherish as a family?

A few years back, we had some visitors stop by a condo we were renting to see if they'd like to take up our lease so that we could move into a home we had purchased. We were away, and a few hours after they visited, Tommy received an email and eagerly opened it, hoping to see an agreement to take over the lease. Instead, the email asked, "Are you guys Catholic?"

The email then went on to say that *they* were Catholic and picked up on a few things around our home. They inquired about parishes in the area that we might have attended. Tommy walked around with a proud smile on his face for weeks after getting that email. They didn't take over the lease, but something about our home made it clear to outsiders that we were

Catholic, and that felt good. (And within a few days, someone else decided that our house was right for them.)

Do we have images of saints around our home? Will visitors see pictures or statues of Mary in our living room, images of the Holy Family in the kids' rooms, or a statue of St. Francis of Assisi in our garden?

One additional thing we do that sends the message to others while keeping saints close to our family is tuck holy cards in the corners of bathroom mirrors. It's great to look at St. Thérèse as we brush our teeth and then get a head start on prayer by flipping the card over to the prayer on the back.

Remember, the Saints Are Real, and They Are Praying for Us

It can be so easy to intellectualize the faith, to know truth in our heads without really embracing that truth in our hearts. Yes, we know that the communion of saints is real. We know our Church teaches us that the saints intercede on our behalf. But do we embrace that truth in the depths of our hearts and souls?

Do we ask for the intercession of St. Anthony, expecting that he's actually hearing us and ready to help us find those missing keys? Do we call out to St. Jude when all hope is lost, believing that he's prepared to take our worries to Jesus? Do we reach out to St. Gerard Majella for a safe pregnancy, feeling deep down that he asks Jesus to keep us safe?

It can be somewhat challenging to answer these questions honestly. Of course we believe in the power of prayer, we tell ourselves, but when life is falling to pieces and we don't know where else to turn, do we really believe in the intercession of the communion of saints?

This is a great place for our kids to jump in and help us. *They really do believe.* They don't question that their guardian angels are there to help them. They don't second-guess that Mary is their mother in heaven, prepared to ask Jesus for everything they need. They believe, and their childlike faith is meant to inspire us to believe just as deeply. So take this opportunity to become childlike in your love of the saints, and allow their example and powerful intercession to push you deeper in your spirituality than ever before.

IT'S A FEAST DAY SOMEWHERE

Living the liturgical calendar

Sitting in Mass with our kids one Pentecost morning, we listened attentively to the readings and homily and realized that we might need to do some explaining over donuts afterward. (This was in the days before we discussed the readings before Mass.) Violent wind inside a locked room? *Tongues* of fire? The apostles speaking in languages that they didn't know so that those listening, no matter what their own native language, could understand them? Oh, and singing "Happy Birthday" to the Church after Mass was over?!?

This all sounded pretty bizarre to the ears of our three children, and the puzzled expressions on their faces made us realize that we don't typically sit around the dinner table chatting about the events commemorated on the feast of Pentecost. We tend to focus on the obvious topics when we talk with our kids about the faith: the Eucharist, the role of Mary in our lives, the importance of the Church. It's impossible to cover *everything*, of course, and that Sunday morning, with the whole Church decked out in red, we found ourselves with a teachable moment on our hands.

We used the feast day as a springboard for discussing with the kids exactly what Pentecost is all about: the wind as the force of the Holy Spirit; the tongues of fire not actually being like the tongues in our mouths but rather the love and power of the Spirit touching Jesus' friends and mother; the ability of the Spirit enabling the apostles to speak in languages they didn't know; the connection of Pentecost to the Sacrament of Confirmation; and recognizing this moment as the "birthday" of the Church because it's the day the apostles embraced and embarked upon the Church's mission to preach the gospel to all creation. It was an awesome moment for our family, an opportunity to explore a foundational New Testament event.

It was also an eye-opening moment for us as parents. We realized the simple power of the liturgical year to help us teach our children the faith in a way that feels natural, as opposed to bringing up random topics over pancakes. Before we jump in and share some of our family's favorite days on the liturgical calendar (not counting Advent and Lent, which deserve and get their own chapters), let's sort out some terms.

A Feast, a Memorial, or a Solemnity?

The feast of the Immaculate Conception. The memorial of St. Blaise. The solemnity of Mary, Mother of God. Why is one a feast, one a memorial, and the other a solemnity?

The term *feast* holds a particular meaning in terms of the hierarchy of celebrations in the Church, but in our everyday conversations, the term often covers the whole gamut of Church celebrations. Most fellow Catholics wouldn't give someone a hard time for calling Pentecost a feast even though it's *technically* a solemnity. But it's worth finding out which is which and why because your kids are probably going to ask you at some point.

A solemnity is the highest ranking of all Church celebrations and typically honors and reveals an important mystery of the faith. The Immaculate Conception, the Most Holy Trinity, All Saints Day, the Most Holy Body and Blood of Christ—these are examples of feasts that would rise to the level of a solemnity. The Church also honors some saints with a solemnity, such as St. Joseph and St. John the Baptist. Solemnities are focused on serious business, and we are likely to find ourselves in a pew on these days. In fact, solemnities are often holy days of obligation, but these vary from country to country.

A feast typically honors a specific important event in Church history or certain special saints. Feasts include the Baptism of Our Lord, the Transfiguration, Our Lady of Guadalupe, the Visitation of the Blessed Virgin Mary, the Holy Family, the Conversion of St. Paul, and the feasts of the apostles.

A memorial would be next up on our hierarchy of important days. Memorials honor those who have lived lives of heroic virtue, deserving of our veneration and recognition. Most of the saints' days we observe are in fact memorials, even though Catholics generally, as noted, lump these days together under the heading of "feast" in everyday usage—for example, the memorial of St. Damian, the memorial of St. Blaise, or St. Kateri Tekakwitha, or St. Joan of Arc, and so on. We may not be obliged to go to Mass on a given memorial but, as we discussed in the previous chapter, such days *always* offer a great opportunity to celebrate in our own little domestic churches, to connect our family to the saints as we learn more about how they can help us lead a holy life.

Let's take a brief look at the liturgical year and explore how we can use liturgical living as a way to teach our kids (and ourselves) what we believe and why we believe it.

—THE SOLEMNITY OF THE EPIPHANY OF THE LORD—

Traditionally January 6; more recently the Sunday between January 2 and 8 in the United States

In the Catholic Church, the Epiphany commemorates the visit of the magi to the baby Jesus. We all know the story of those three wise men who came bearing gifts of gold, frankincense, and myrrh to pay homage to the newborn king:

And behold, the star that they had seen at its rising preceded them, until it came and stopped over the place where the child was. They were overjoyed at seeing the star, and on entering the house they saw the child with Mary his mother. They prostrated themselves and did him homage. (Matthew 2:9-11)

The message of the Epiphany, however, and the roots of this solemnity go deeper. According to the *Catechism of the Catholic Church*:

The *Epiphany* is the manifestation of Jesus as Messiah of Israel, Son of God and Savior of the world. . . . In the magi, representatives of the neighboring pagan religions, the Gospel sees the first-fruits of the nations, who welcome the good news of salvation through the Incarnation. . . . Their coming means that pagans can discover Jesus and worship him as Son of God and Savior of the world only by turning toward the Jews and receiving from them the messianic promise as contained in the Old Testament. (CCC, 528; cf. John 4:22; Matthew 2:4-6)

To help connect our children to this solemnity, we've made an effort to go outside before bedtime and look up at the stars. If you decide to do this, bring a flashlight and a Bible along, or fire up a Bible website, and as you stand under the stars, read the passage from the Gospel of Matthew about the magi following the star to Bethlehem. Standing in awe under the night sky is a great way to help your kids enter into the events we celebrate this day.

Another way to observe the Epiphany is through an old tradition lately brought into prominence by social media: the chalking of the door to the home, followed by a prayer of blessing. You may have seen the following, for example, written above the main door to a house: "20 + C + M + B + 19." Have you wondered what this meant? Here you go:

The "20" and "19" indicate the current year, and the C, M, and B refer to the traditional names of the magi: Caspar, Melchior, and Balthasar. In addition, the C, M, and B represent the Latin phrase *Christus mansionem benedicat*, which means, "May Christ bless this house."

This is a fun tradition that will not only help you mark the feast and pray a blessing on your house and family, but also help you keep Christ in mind as you come and go over the course of the year. You can find brief blessings and appropriate Scripture passages online that will help you lead your family through this chalking of the lintel and blessing of the home.

And it wouldn't be a solemnity without a sweet treat, right? A king cake—also used to mark Mardi Gras—is an appropriate way to celebrate the feast. Traditionally, little trinkets are mixed into the batter or, alternatively, a little crown to mark the one who gets that slice as king of the festivities.

—THE FEAST OF THE CHAIR OF ST. PETER—

February 22

It doesn't get much more Catholic than having an entire feast day dedicated to a chair! In reality, the feast of the Chair of St. Peter is about much more than the *literal* chair, although there *is* a literal chair in Rome called the chair of St. Peter. (It's a relic enclosed in a bronze chair that was designed by Bernini and is on display at the far end of St. Peter's Basilica.) Liturgically, however, the term refers to the authority of the first pope and his successors. As such, the feast presents a fantastic opportunity for families to learn more about the papacy and its role in the Church and in our lives.

The Latin word *cathedra*, from which we derive our word *cathedral*, means "seat." In a general audience on the feast of the Chair of St. Peter in 2006, Pope Benedict XVI noted,

> "Cathedra" literally means the established seat of the Bishop, placed in the mother church of a diocese which for this reason is known as a "cathedral"; it is the symbol of the Bishop's authority. . . .
>
> . . . [T]he Chair of the Bishop of Rome represents not only his service to the Roman community but also his mission as guide of the entire People of God.
>
> Celebrating the "Chair" of Peter, therefore, as we are doing today, means attributing a strong spiritual significance to it and recognizing it as a privileged sign of the love of God, the eternal Good Shepherd, who wanted to gather his whole Church and lead her on the path of salvation.[8]

We can celebrate this feast in a spirit of gratitude that Jesus saw fit to leave shepherds here on earth to guide us as we work hard to stay on the path to heaven.

If you want your kids to feel more connected to the papacy, this would be a good day to have them write a letter to the pope. When our son Paul was four years old and feeling a little peeved that Mass lasted an entire hour, he informed us that he'd be writing to the pope requesting that Mass be shortened to a more bearable time as soon as possible. His letter—he dictated it, and we mailed it on his behalf—doesn't seem to have had an impact on the length of Mass, but writing a letter can help kids realize that the pope is a real person guiding our Church through the authority given to him by Christ.

It also seems pretty reasonable to have your kids make a chair out of sweet treats, something similar to a gingerbread house. They can marvel at their beautiful creation and then chow down.

—THE SOLEMNITY OF ST. JOSEPH, SPOUSE OF THE BLESSED VIRGIN MARY—

March 19

The most often overlooked member of the Holy Family, St. Joseph most definitely deserves some love from our families when his feast day comes up on the calendar. He's the foster father of Jesus, the spouse of Mary, and a fine example of what it means to be a good husband, father, and man, in a world that can often be hostile to faith and families.

As the patron of the universal Church and of fathers, carpenters, travelers, social justice, and a happy death, St. Joseph surely has a special connection to each of us. Scripture tells us that he followed the inspiration of the Lord without question (as in the Gospel of Matthew 1:24: "When Joseph awoke, he did as the angel of the Lord had commanded him and took his wife into his home"). Teaching our children about his example as a humble and patient man who always followed the call of God, even when it was hard, is sure to help them understand what it means to be holy.

Putting together a St. Joseph's altar (also known as a St. Joseph's table) is a popular way to mark his feast. Create a special space and adorn it with different items that relate to the saint, such as holy cards, woodworking tools, and lilies, as well as different foods that have some religious significance or are related in some way to this humble saint. One traditional approach is to place the items on steps leading up to a statue of St. Joseph on the altar, and then surround those with the food items.

In Italy, families would invite the less fortunate in their neighborhoods to come over and enjoy the St. Joseph's altar. It was a way of reaching out, helping others, and bringing the community more closely together. The origins of this custom are obscure but are said to go back to a famine in Sicily that came to an end after the Sicilians prayed to St. Joseph.

There are many sources online to help you prepare a St. Joseph's altar, either on a small scale for your family or, for the adventuresome, for a parish-wide event in honor of St. Joseph.

Either way, spend some time in family prayer before the altar, asking for St. Joseph's intercession.

On a much simpler level, you can wear red clothing to honor St. Joseph's connection to Italian culture. You can also add fava beans to the menu. They're considered "lucky"—or blessed, we would say!—because they kept the Sicilians alive during the famine.

—THE SOLEMNITY OF CORPUS CHRISTI (THE BODY AND BLOOD OF CHRIST)—
The Thursday after Trinity Sunday, observed on the following Sunday in the United States

The Body and Blood of Our Lord and Savior Jesus Christ. The source and summit of our Catholic faith. We talk *a lot* about the Eucharist, the mystery behind the miracle of the altar, the love that Jesus demonstrated by giving himself to us in the Eucharist, and the immense respect we owe to the Blessed Sacrament. But once every year, we push that reverence even further.

On the solemnity of Corpus Christi, also known as the solemnity of the Most Holy Body and Blood of Christ, we thank God for feeding us with his own Body and Blood and for the grace he offers us through the Eucharist. It is indeed our true food and true drink, and it helps sustain our relationship with him. So how can we elevate our appreciation of the Eucharist even more when this solemnity comes around?

In the United States, many parishes hold Eucharistic processions on this great day, and we highly recommend taking your kids if your parish or a nearby parish does this. Catholic children participate in the Eucharist weekly (or more often) within the walls of the church, but they will have a totally different experience in a procession, walking along the town sidewalk behind the priest, who holds Our Lord's Body in a monstrance. We don't often pray and witness to the faith in public these days, and the Eucharistic procession can be very powerful for adults and kids alike.

Stopping by the adoration chapel at a local parish is another way to tap into the grace flowing from this solemnity. It can be intimidating to enter that sacred silence with children, but they are welcome there. Bring them before the Blessed Sacrament on the altar, and ask Jesus to come into their hearts and the hearts of your entire family. Ask him to lead you all away from sin and into a deeper relationship with him.

—MEMORIAL OF OUR LADY OF SORROWS—
September 15

All of us experience sorrow and trouble, and during the most difficult times, we can feel alone, even abandoned by God. How could God, his mother, or the saints understand the pain and suffering we are going through at any given moment? The memorial of Our Lady of Sorrows reminds us that Mary knows what it's like to walk through dark times, and she's here to show us how to maintain faith and hope even during the darkest moments.

This feast dates back to at least the twelfth century, but it only made it onto the official calendar in 1482, under the title of Our Lady of Compassion. The feast reminds us that Mary experienced pain in her life—from the prophecy of Simeon that a sword would pierce her heart to the crucifixion and burial of her beloved only Son. Through it all, she maintained hope in God and his plan. We can look to Mary and ask for her intercession when we find it difficult to trust, hope, and continue on.

As on the solemnity of St. Joseph, this is a great day to put together a family altar. Set aside a special place; adorn it with flowers, holy cards, and similar reminders of the mother of Jesus; and gather the family there for prayer. Honor this woman who said yes to God, knowing full well that her yes would mean personal suffering.

You can observe this solemnity by meditating on the seven sorrows of Mary as you pray the Rosary: the prophecy of Simeon, the flight into Egypt, the loss of the child Jesus in Jerusalem, meeting Jesus on his way to Calvary, the crucifixion and death of Jesus, Jesus being taken down from the cross, and the burial of Jesus. You can also pray the Servite Rosary—the specific prayers centered on Mary's suffering can be found online—to mark the day. Contemplating the sorrows Mary endured in order to bring Jesus and his salvation to the world is a good reminder for us all that Mary, although she was highly favored by God, suffered and can sympathize with our suffering.

While there may not be a traditional dessert associated with this feast, heart-shaped cookies seem like a no-brainer.

—MEMORIAL OF THE
HOLY GUARDIAN ANGELS—

October 2

Every night before we go to sleep, our family joins in a prayer to our guardian angels, asking for their protection, begging for their assistance, and seeking their guidance as we walk along the journey of our lives. We often speak of these angels and the fact that we each have an angel appointed to watch over us and help us. Jesus alluded to the protection of these heavenly beings when he said, "See that you do not despise one of these little ones, for I say to you that their angels in heaven always look upon the face of my heavenly Father" (Matthew 18:10).

This feast day, authorized by Pope Paul V in 1608, is a great day to impress on your children that they have a member of the heavenly host keeping an eye on them 24/7 and empowering them to make the right choices. In a letter to a friend, St. Padre Pio wrote powerfully about the companion we have in our angel:

How consoling it is to know that we have a spirit who, from the womb to the tomb, never leaves us even for an instant, not even when we dare to sin. And this heavenly spirit guides and protects us like a friend, a brother.

But it is very consoling to know that this angel prays unceasingly for us, and offers God all of our good actions, our thoughts, and our desires, if they are pure.

Oh! For goodness' sake, don't forget this invisible companion, ever present, ever disposed to listen to us and even more ready to console us. Oh, wonderful intimacy! Oh, blessed companionship![9]

Considering that amazing companionship, that incredible guidance our angels offer, why not sit down with your kiddos to write a thank-you card to their guardian angels. Perhaps there was a time where they felt they were protected from danger or a time where they felt like everything worked out when it seemed at first like it might not—all great reasons to say thanks to our heavenly guides, who are with us from womb to tomb.

And when it comes to food, you can't go wrong with angel-hair pasta for dinner and angel food cake for dessert!

—ALL SOULS DAY—
November 2

Most of us are pretty familiar with All Saints Day, celebrated on November 1, but what about All Souls Day, the holy day set aside for remembering the dead? The Church asks us to remember in prayer not only members of our own family who have passed away but also members of the human family we have never known and who may have no one praying for their souls.

On this day, we can share stories about family members who have died but, most important, we should pray for their souls, that they may receive the glorious reward waiting for them in heaven. We ought to pray for the souls of the faithful departed every day, but especially on this day that the Church has set aside to remember those who have gone before us.

Consider observing this day by visiting a cemetery where a loved one is laid to rest or attending Mass to pray for the dead; sometimes parishes even mark the day by celebrating Mass at the local Catholic cemetery. Bring out old photo albums, and talk about relatives who have passed away. Prepare some of the foods that remind you of them.

It's another opportunity to set up an altar, this time with mementos of those family members. Pictures, favorite foods, items that remind us of them—these are all great ways to remember that they have not died in a final sense but are still alive, still care about us, and are still connected to us in a very real way.

And, of course, aside from those favorite foods, we can celebrate the day with some foods that may be new to us, such as soul cake, *pan de los muertos*, or the Italian dish Eggs in Purgatory. There are plenty of traditionally appropriate foods to mark the feast.

The Church gives us the liturgical calendar to help us structure our year, learn about the faith, and pass on its truths to our children. With traditions from our childhood or with new traditions, let's take advantage of these built-in feasts to strengthen our families in faith and establish ourselves in the rhythm of the Catholic year.

SEVEN

PREPARING FOR CHRISTMAS

Making Advent a time they'll never forget

A few weeks after Paul turned two, we went to a birthday party for a friend's five-year-old. This kid was very into Star Wars and so of course, he had a Star Wars–themed party. His parents pulled out all of the stops. They had games and a Jedi training course and even Darth Vader made an appearance to challenge the kids to a lightsaber battle.

And there was a piñata! Paul had never seen a piñata before but because he was the youngest kid at the party, he got to swing first. He didn't quite get the point of hitting this thing with a plastic bat . . . until an older kid gave it the final smack, it burst open, and candy rained down.

Let's just say we do not throw elaborate birthday parties for our kids. Nevertheless, Paul was enthralled, and he immediately started to plan his next birthday, which was about 341 days away. For the rest of the year, he planned his party, talking about piñatas nonstop and making and remaking his birthday present wish list.

As Paul has gotten older, not much has changed in terms of his excitement about his birthday. He has also made a hobby of preparing his Christmas wish list months in advance. This may be a completely normal thing for a kid to do, but Paul's lists stand in total contrast to his brother James'. To illustrate.

A few years ago, California was in its seventh year of a terrible drought. It was the beginning of December, and we had received less than an inch of rain over the entire year. Needless to say, people talked about the drought all the time, and naturally the kids overheard these conversations. They talked in school about water conservation too.

All this concern was evident when looking over the boys' Christmas lists that year. James asked for rain so that the drought would end, apples, hugs and kisses, a quarter, and a ball that he could toss around with Andy. Karen's heart melted.

Paul stood wide-eyed, with a huge smile on his face, as he handed his list over. It was overflowing with the typical kid desires: candy, rollerblades, nunchucks, and the like.

Although Paul's list may have been more typical than James's, it troubled Karen that Paul was *so* focused on the gift-giving aspect of Christmas rather than the beautiful meaning of the season. Then, while digging through a box of memorabilia from her childhood, she discovered a Christmas list from when she was about eight years old. It, too, was overflowing with the desires of a typical eight-year-old girl in the '80s, topped off by the still exciting Get in Shape Girl exercise set.

Decades earlier and halfway across the globe, the boy who would become Pope Benedict pulled together a Christmas list a bit more on track with our Catholic faith. At age seven, Joseph Ratzinger's list stated, "I promise I'll be good," and he requested three items in exchange for his good behavior: a vestment for when he played Mass with his brother Georg; the Mass missal translated into German, so that he could understand the Latin; and a specific image of the Sacred Heart. Wow! Not sure how any of us could compete with that! He must have never seen Get in Shape Girl.

No matter if your kids' lists look like Joseph Ratzinger's or Paul's or are somewhere in between, you can prepare their hearts for Christmas in a way that will make the season stand out. In the last two chapters, we covered the many ways in which Catholics can celebrate. In this chapter and the next, we'll talk about how to prepare for the biggest celebrations on the Catholic calendar: Christmas and Easter. We'll start with Advent, the run-up to Christmas.

Preparation, Not Party

Many people put up the Christmas tree, decorate, and hang the lights outside the house the weekend after Thanksgiving. And as Christmas draws near, our calendars become filled with party invitations, family get-togethers, lunch parties at work, and Secret Santa gift exchanges—all scheduled smack dab in the middle of

Advent. Yet according to the website of the United States Conference of Catholic Bishops, "The Advent season is a time of preparation that directs our hearts and minds to Christ's second coming at the end of time and also to the anniversary of the Lord's birth on Christmas."[10]

Preparation, not party. Patiently waiting, not celebrating ahead of time.

With all that's going on well before December 25, it can be difficult to maintain this perspective. So, without withdrawing from the world and without keeping our homes dark during the lead-up to one of the holiest days of the year, what steps can we take to maintain and drive home this attitude of reflection and preparation during Advent? We have a few ideas for you.

Confession

We're going to go ahead and get the hard part out of the way: going to Confession at the beginning of Advent is probably the best way to prepare for the birth of Christ. Confession frees us from our sins and burdens and opens us up to the grace God is prepared to pour out during this powerful season. We spend so much time getting the house ready for visitors—cleaning, cooking, hiding the unfolded laundry in an already overstuffed closet—why not make the effort to get *ourselves* ready?

Consider going to Confession a couple of times during Advent—once at the beginning and then again during regular Saturday hours or during your parish penance service. Going to Confession on the regular during Advent helps us, of course, but it also sends a powerful message to our children. Let's face it: our children are not going to see the value in Confession unless they see it happening before their eyes. If they see us getting to church to admit our wrongs and hear us talking about how good it feels to know we have received the forgiveness of Christ and his Church for our sins, they are going to long for the gift of grace available in this beautiful sacrament.

On the flip side, if we haven't been to Confession in six years because we don't see its value, we can be certain that our kids will grow up to feel the same way. If it has been six years (or even thirty-six years), never fear. There is no better time than Advent to get back on the ball with Confession. And remember: the priest has heard it all before. Really, he has!

Actually Use That Advent Wreath

The Advent wreath offers families an opportunity to join in prayer together as they journey toward Christmas. Each of the four candles in the wreath symbolizes a different aspect of getting ready: three purple candles for prayer, penance, and the preparatory sacrifices and good works we undertake during this time, and one rose-colored candle representing rejoicing, because it marks the midway point of Advent. As we light a new candle each week, according to the US bishops, we experience "the expectation and hope surrounding our Lord's first coming into the world and the anticipation of his second coming to judge the living and the dead."[11]

And as Catholics, you had better believe that to get us up and running, we have readings and prayers to go along with the lighting of each candle. Between Scripture verses appropriate to the season, prayers, and stories we can share around the wreath each night of Advent, our families will come to understand the preparatory spirit that is central to the season.

Jesus in the Manger: Now or Later?

As with so many things in the Catholic world, for better or for worse, there is a great deal of debate around the little baby Jesus and his presence in the nativity scene during Advent.

It may surprise you to learn that St. Francis of Assisi is credited with creating the very first nativity scene, back in 1223. (Is there anything St. Francis didn't do?!) Within a hundred years of St. Francis' initial creation, every church in Italy had a nativity scene during the Advent and Christmas seasons, and it didn't take long for the tradition to spread throughout all of Christendom and even into the secular world.

Now to the pressing issue of the baby Jesus. Should Jesus be present in the manger from the start, when we set up our nativity set, to focus people on the reason for the season? Or should he be left out of the manger scene until Christmas Day, to underscore that we are in a time of preparation? Catholics typically respect the both/and approach rather than the either/or style of addressing issues, and we think it should be no different when it comes to Jesus in the manger in the middle of December.

As parents who help children work through difficult choices multiple times per day, we love to pull together pro and con lists to help us navigate decisions. So . . .

Pro for putting Jesus in early: a great reminder of the reason for the season. Con for putting Jesus in early: it can hinder the spirit of preparation.

Pro for putting Jesus in early: it completes the look of the nativity scene. Con for putting Jesus in early: having an empty manger can spark conversations about why we've chosen to temporarily omit Jesus.

Pro for putting Jesus in early: he's so darn cute (and if you keep him out, you're likely to forget where you stored him). Con for putting Jesus in early: he hasn't actually arrived yet, so in order to be faithful to the liturgy, we must have him wait in the wings.

The tally comes out even. And so, as with most things we discuss in this book, you have to do what's best for your family and not worry about what the neighbors think!

Praying the O Antiphons

With the rise of social media, Catholics have learned about another Advent tradition that most of us were not familiar with: praying the O Antiphons. The O Antiphons are typically sung or recited at vespers (evening prayer) over the last seven days of Advent. They are also used as the *Alleluia* verses on those same days at Mass.

These beautiful little additions to Advent are referred to as the O Antiphons because each begins with "O" and contains a different title of Jesus as reflected in Scripture. Included in this awesome list are "O Wisdom," "O Lord," "O Root of Jesse," "O Key of David," "O Dayspring," "O King of Nations," and "O With Us Is God."

When you add the O Antiphons to your family prayers in the final week of Advent, or when you hear one sung before the Gospel at Mass, you know you are getting really, *really* close to Christmas.

A Spirit of Giving

In a season that has become jam-packed with shopping and the potential for spoiling children rotten, it's important for parents to instill a spirit of giving in their children. In order to help the kids feel part of our charitable giving, every Advent we put together a list of charities and ask the kids to select one that we should support as a family. We explain what each charity does and why it's important to support it. We then remind them that we don't have an infinite supply of money, and we'll have to make a sacrifice somewhere in our budget in order to come up with the money to give away.

We often focus on charities that specifically help children. When our kids hear that there are kids just like them who are homeless or terminally ill and who have no toys to call their own, it helps them put their own lives into context and to appreciate the gifts God has given our family.

One Christmas we distributed gifts to children and families through our local Catholic Worker ministry. To be clear, we didn't actually do something as nice as buying or wrapping the gifts, but we showed up with the kids to help hand out gifts to the families in need. We watched as each of our children gave a child their age a gift, perhaps the only gift that child would receive that year.

We talked on the way home about how excited these kids were to receive a single small gift. The experience really hit home for our kids. It helped them understand how blessed they are and how thankful they should be.

O Christmas Tree, O Christmas Tree!

When he was a kid, few things got Tommy's heart fluttering as did watching his dad bring in the boxes of decorations to adorn the Christmas tree. They'd go through the boxes and pull out ornaments they hadn't seen all year, fawning over them as if they were friends not seen since college. The pinball machine ornament that made cool sounds, the colorful bubblers that now seem to be illegal because of the fire risk, the statue of Santa kneeling before the crib in Bethlehem—all of it meant Christmas was coming.

Few things warm the heart more than seeing a glowing Christmas tree through the front window of a home. Something about it makes everyone feel happy, friendly, and as if there's hope that everything in life is going to be okay. Would it surprise you to learn that there is a tradition, part historic and part legend, that gives the Christmas tree a Catholic origin?

The story starts with St. Boniface, an Englishman who became a missionary to Germany in the eighth century. After preaching the gospel successfully for a time, Boniface went to Rome to consult with the pope. On his return to Germany, he came across a group of pagans who had gathered, during the winter solstice, to sacrifice a young man under an oak tree sacred to their god Thor. Boniface grabbed an axe and chopped down the sacred oak, to the horror of the pagans, who expected the god to take revenge.

This much is attested to in very early accounts of Boniface's life. The rest of the story, however, is conjecture, though it does capture a sense of the meaning behind the Christmas tree.

After felling the oak, the story goes, Boniface then preached the gospel to the pagans, who were still in shock, and pointed to a tiny fir tree standing behind the now destroyed oak. "Boniface was familiar with the popular custom of taking an evergreen plant into the house in winter," we read in *L'Osservatore Romano*, the Vatican newspaper. And so he "asked everyone to take home a fir tree." Just like that, a tradition was born. The article goes on to say that "this tree signifies peace, and as an evergreen it also symbolizes immortality; with its top pointing upwards, it additionally indicates heaven, the dwelling place of God."[12]

Whether the origins of this custom are rooted in history, lore, or a combination of both, all these years later, we still set up our Christmas trees and decorate them in honor of the Christ child.

Jesse Tree

The Jesse tree is a lovely way to help families learn more about the ancestors of Christ and the beautiful stories of the Old Testament leading up to the virgin birth. It is based on a passage in Isaiah:

A shoot shall sprout from the stump of Jesse,
and from his roots a bud shall blossom. (Isaiah 11:1)

Jesus, of course, is the shoot. The Jesse tree devotion and craft involve not only learning about his ancestors—the people in his family tree—but also making ornaments to represent their stories and attaching them to the tree. The tree can be an actual tree branch or can be constructed from felt or construction paper. By the end of Advent, a Jesse tree is crowded with beautiful ornaments that symbolize those Old Testament stories.

You can buy premade Jesse trees or make your own, as Karen did. She spent weeks painstakingly cutting and gluing the felt tree to a felt background and making the ornaments that would be added each day as we discussed each biblical story. Then she had to figure out a way to keep it out of the kids' hands until it was time to celebrate the devotion!

The ornaments were beautiful, of course, but the main takeaway from all her hard work was the opportunity they created for all of us to learn as a family. Sure, we knew the stories of Adam, Moses, Noah, and a few others, but when it came to the ornaments for Hezekiah, Habakkuk, and Nehemiah, for example, we had to admit we had no idea what their stories were about. This made the Jesse tree an exciting activity for our family every night of Advent, because we were exploring Scripture together and learning together. Karen's hard work making the tree and its decorations has given our family something to enjoy every Advent.

Starry Night Nativity Scene

Our oldest son came home from faith formation one afternoon with an awesome new Advent tradition. He had made a simple nativity scene: paper cutouts of the Holy Family and the manger. These were glued to a piece of black construction paper, on which he had drawn a couple of stars in the night sky.

"My teacher said we should draw a star in the night sky every time we do something nice for God, our family, or someone else," he explained. He was excited about the idea of adding a star every time he led the family in a prayer, jumped up and did what his mom asked without a complaint, or held the door open for a stranger on the way into the library.

The goal? "My teacher said that by the time Christmas arrives, the entire sky should be full of stars!" It turned out to be a fun activity for the whole family, helping us keep our priorities straight during the Advent season.

What to Do with Santa

What to do about Santa Claus seems to be a main topic of debate during the Advent and Christmas seasons. Jolly Old St. Nick, Kris Kringle, Father Christmas—whatever you call him, Catholics and other Christians have been debating his place in their families' celebrations for generations, and the discussion shows no sign of letting up.

There are two camps on this issue. First, you have the anti-Santa crowd, the group who believe Santa has no place in

Christmas. "We need to focus on Jesus" is the main argument on this side of the debate. There's also serious concern about parents "lying" to their children, pushing them to believe something, only to later admit that it isn't true.

On the other side of the debate is the pro-Santa crowd, the group that loves the "magic" of Santa and his reindeer. We've known parents who've left sooty footprints by the fireplace and managed to put reindeer tracks in the snow on the roof. Some families joke that even the grown children have to believe in Santa in order to receive gifts.

We have gone back and forth over this in our house ever since our first child was born, with Tommy generally being pro-Santa and Karen being anti-Santa. We settled on the approach of not really being anti-Santa but also not overdoing him. And as our kids got a little older, we started to think harder about how we wanted to handle Santa's place in our family's Christmas experience.

One solution we really liked was having each of us be Santa for someone else, transforming the tradition into something focused on helping others. This allowed us to recognize that there were attributes of Santa that we admired (a spirit of giving without the expectation of receiving in return, helping others, and so forth) and to push toward taking on those attributes ourselves to help us reach out to others. We wanted our children to embrace the idea of helping those less fortunate, to share their blessings with others, and to carry on the Santa tradition in that way rather than focusing on how someone would be slinking down our chimney on Christmas Eve night.

No matter where you stand on the Santa debate, take a deep breath and be cool with whatever the family in the pew next to you is doing. There is no sin in maintaining the story of Santa Claus and no sin in deciding Santa isn't a good fit for your family. Instead of getting upset or talking about how your way is better than someone else's, take a cue from jolly old St. Nick: eat a cookie and be happy!

Blessings Jar

This family tradition is in reality a yearlong effort, but we wrap it up during the Christmas season, so we're going to tell you about it here.

As a Catholic family, we try to live in a spirit of thankfulness and to impress that on our kids. While it's easy to recommend "counting our blessings" as a family, it can be a lot more difficult to make it a part of our routine. A few years back, we kicked off a family tradition of a blessings jar to help make it easier.

A large glass jar sits on top of our dining room cabinet, next to a handful of paper strips and a pen. Throughout the year we encourage everyone to jot down blessings they experience and toss the strips in the jar. On New Year's Eve, we pull our blessings out one by one and take turns reading them, with the whole family gathered around the table.

It's inspiring to recall all the blessings we have received, some of which we might have forgotten. They range from serious blessings—like having affordable health care when we needed it or the healing of a family member struggling with illness—all the way down to the simple, everyday blessings we typically overlook—like how Andrew said a word in his cute little three-year-old voice, or that one afternoon the boys somehow figured out how to not to fight with each other.

We parents enjoy reading through blessings from the year but not half as much as the kids enjoy it. "Oh, yeah! I totally forgot about that time Grandpa let us eat our ice cream *before* dinner!"

EIGHT

PREPARING FOR EASTER

Praying, fasting, giving—and rejoicing

Lent was, and is, and forever shall be, Tommy's favorite season of the liturgical year. Sure, Catholics are great when it comes to feasting and celebration, but when it comes to the whole sack-cloth-and-ashes thing, we are absolute champions. Giving things up for Lent has become a cultural phenomenon, but we Catholics still strive, as a group, to do it right.

One year, Tommy's coworker mentioned that she gave up ice cream every year, only to be befuddled when Tommy remarked that he was giving up his pillow.

"Why would you give up your pillow?!" she asked.

"Because," he said, he liked to do things "the hard way."

Looking back, Tommy realizes he probably could have handled the situation with a little less "Catholic superiority." But we're all growing day by day, right?

While giving up your pillow, or hot showers, or (gasp) coffee might be a choice that appeals to you, the ultimate Lenten challenge for families is figuring out how to incorporate prayer, fasting, and almsgiving in a way that matches your particular family dynamics.

Prayer

First and foremost on our Lenten to-do list should be prayer. We often hear the advice "Instead of giving something up for Lent, consider taking something on," and when it comes to prayer, this advice is pretty spot on.

Confession

We've mentioned Confession many times in this book, but who's counting, right? We've hammered home how important this grace-packed sacrament is and how parents ought to set an example for their children by going regularly. We've done this because we want to highlight how valuable and healing Confession is.

In chapter four, we talked about the four most important things we can say to someone we love: *please, thank you, I'm sorry,* and *I love you.* In Confession we say these four things to God, and he says them directly back to us.

We say,

Please, God, help me overcome my sinful inclinations.

Thank you for offering your grace and forgiveness to me in this sacrament.

I'm sorry for offending you . . .

. . . because *I love you.*

In return he calls to us,

Please never tire of coming to me for mercy, love, and grace.

Thank you for being willing to repent and return to me.

I'm sorry you have to experience pain, suffering, and doubt . . .

. . . because *I love you.*

Lenten Prayer Chain

As a family, we sometimes make a paper chain to mark off the days until a special event. Our kids absolutely love this practice. They rip off a link per day until they arrive at their birthday, Christmas, a family vacation, and so forth. We've discovered that making a chain to mark the forty days of Lent is a great way to keep kids focused on the season of preparation for Easter Sunday.

We turn this practice into a prayer chain by writing an intention on each strip of paper. Every morning we rip off a link in the chain, read the intention, and then go about the day keeping that intention in mind. A prayer for the family, a prayer for friends, a prayer for our pope, priests, our world—any and all needs are welcome. Encouraging everyone to focus on the intention together helps to foster not only an attitude of prayer throughout Lent, but also the very Catholic idea of praying throughout the entire day, allowing everything we do to be marked by prayer.

When the kids have to do something at school that they don't particularly enjoy, they can offer it up for that day's intention. When Mom or Dad has to sit through a particularly boring and seemingly pointless meeting at work, they can do the same. When the family comes together to pray in the morning, before meals, or at bedtime, they can keep the intention in mind.

A prayer chain is a great way to remind the entire family that Lent isn't just about sacrificing that sweet treat after dinner. It's a time of prayerful reflection and a constant reminder that we rely on God for all our needs.

Going One Small Step Further

When we reflected on the Rosary in chapter 4, we talked about "getting there" in small steps: starting off with just the Our Father and three Hail Marys, moving on to completing one mystery, and slowly but surely getting to the place where we can pray the entire Rosary with the family. This practical approach will move a family toward praying the Rosary together and also help them in general to grow in faith.

So often we decide we need to do *something* to deepen our faith, and then we go all in without planning, without taking it slow. We decide to start praying the Liturgy of the Hours and feel as though we have to pray every single hour—even those middle-of-the-night ones. If we miss a prayer for any reason, we feel like a failure and want to give up on the whole endeavor.

For Tommy, who loves to jump in on frequent attempts to improve his life, this all-or-nothing approach tends to lead to a cycle of hope, failure, and regret. He's learned that he has to be okay with taking small steps toward a concrete goal, while being okay with setbacks or having to slow down. He learned this life lesson—we both learned it—when we were teaching Paul how to read.

Now, our oldest son, James, loved his reading lessons. He could tear through a story without taking breaks. When we embarked on the journey with Paul, we wanted things to go the same way. They didn't.

Paul struggled with reading, and we became disenchanted with the entire process. The nightly power struggles and frustration continued until Karen decided that *he didn't have to go at the prescribed pace*. We split his lessons in half, allowing ourselves to be okay with the process taking twice as long. And Paul flourished.

It was a lightbulb moment for us, one that we try to carry into different areas of our lives. We don't have to go from zero to one hundred immediately. We need to be willing to go at the pace that eventually gets the job done.

So as we suggested earlier when talking about finding your way back to Mass, consider your faith journey and that of your family. Talk with a priest. Figure out where you are.

If you enter the season of Lent never attending Mass, try attending once per month. If you go once per month now, go twice. If you go to Mass every Sunday, try picking up one daily Mass per week. You don't have to go all in and start showing up for Mass three times a day in a mantilla with candles in hand., but you can take one step closer to heaven by taking one small step here on earth.

The same holds true with your family's prayer life. If you aren't praying as a family at all, try entering Lent with the goal of saying grace before dinner throughout the season. If you enter Lent only praying before dinner and at bedtime, try adding a prayer before the day gets started. The point is, find something that feels like one extra step, and add that on to what you're already doing.

We all have room to improve when it comes to our prayer life; we all have room to grow. But we have to remember that growth takes time. Set small goals. Don't beat yourself up when you have setbacks. Slowly but surely move your family step-by-step toward a deeper faith, a deeper appreciation of Lent, and understanding the why behind this season of preparation.

Fasting

Yes, we're sorry, but we are here to remind you that we are still called to fast. Fasting has been an essential part of the spiritual life throughout Catholic history. When the Gospel of Matthew speaks of Jesus fasting, we see both his example of fasting *and* his very human nature: "He fasted for forty days and forty nights, and afterwards he was hungry" (Matthew 4:2).

We may not be called to fast for forty days and forty nights as Jesus did, but our Lenten fast is based on his example. The saints through the ages have also reminded us of the importance of saying no to our body's desires through fasting:

Fasting purifies the soul. It lifts up the mind, and it brings the body into subjection to the spirit. It makes the heart contrite and humble, scatters the clouds of desire, puts out the flames of lust and enkindles the true light of chastity.

—St. Augustine[13]

For we fast for three purposes: (1) to restrain the desires of the flesh; (2) to raise the mind to contemplate sublime things; (3) to make satisfaction for our sins. These are good and noble things, and so fasting is virtuous.

—St. Thomas Aquinas[14]

God hides the prize of eternal glory in our mortifications and in the victory of ourselves, which we always strive for with great gentleness.

—St. Jane Frances de Chantal[15]

Today's spiritual giants also speak of the value, grace, and blessings that come with a good fast. Pope Benedict XVI said, "The ultimate goal of fasting is to help each one of us . . . to make the complete gift of self to God."[16]

Nevertheless, fasting can be hard, intimidating, and an opportunity to feel like a failure if we can't pull it off. This was Tommy's experience.

Tommy took up fasting during his freshman year of college. He routinely went through Ash Wednesday and Good Friday without a single crumb of food. He felt like a huge success (that's the sin of pride, for those playing along at home). Slowly but surely, his ability to fast in this way lessened. By the time we had James, Tommy would come home from work after fasting all day and have to lie down. He would be totally stripped of a single ounce of energy—he even threw up from the lack of food. This continued each time he fasted until Karen finally said enough was enough. It wasn't fair for Tommy to come home and be unable to help out simply for the sake of feeling pious. Tommy realized that he needed to tweak his fasting routine and that this was okay. The daylong fast turned into a breakfast-and-lunch fast with a reasonable dinner.

Everything went fine physically, but the inclination to feel like a failure crept in, which led to some soul-searching. It came down to looking at why Tommy was fasting in the first place. Was fasting throughout the day some sort of trophy to be earned? If so, that was a fast offered up for entirely the wrong reason. A far less restrictive fast, done for the right reasons, was much more appropriate."

Karen, when she took up fasting, came to a stark realization. She saw that while most of us can end a fast when we want, with whatever food we want, in whatever amount we want, many people go hungry because of poverty, war, and other atrocities. For Karen, fasting opened up an understanding of and love for those whose fasting is involuntary.

The United States Conference of Catholic Bishops' website lists the official guidelines for Lenten fasting:

> For members of the Latin Catholic Church, the norms on fasting are obligatory from age 18 until age 59. When fasting,

a person is permitted to eat one full meal, as well as two smaller meals that together are not equal to a full meal.[17]

This isn't that difficult, true, but one value of its lack of difficulty is that we are able to stay focused on the reason for fasting: to unite our sacrifice with the sacrifice of Christ on the cross.

Getting the Kids Involved

Although fasting is not required before the age of eighteen and abstaining from meat before the age of fourteen, fasting as a family can help kids start to grasp the value of giving up something good for the sake of something greater. Operation Rice Bowl can help you get creative as you do this.

Operation Rice Bowl is an initiative of Catholic Relief Services designed to help us tithe during Lent (we'll discuss this under almsgiving). But did you know that Operation Rice Bowl also offers recipes from around the world that use ingredients available in American grocery stores? The recipes are all simple and meatless—sacrificial in their simplicity but often delicious.

Talk with your kids about giving up the mac and cheese, chicken nuggets, and burrito nights that typically adorn your calendar. Review some Operation Rice Bowl recipes with them, and then go for something that puts the family in tune with our sisters and brothers around the world. Lablabi soup from Iraq? Let's do it! Sopa de queso from Nicaragua? We're in! Bean cakes from Burkina Faso? We'll take seconds! The next time Lent rolls around, be sure to grab that Rice Bowl after Mass and head on over to the local market for everything you need to make ifisashi, pupusas, and injera with atkilt wat!

Speaking of abstaining from meat during the Lenten season, we want to take a moment to put in a plug for your local parish fish fry. You know it's there. Maybe you haven't been in forever. Make this the Lent when that changes.

The fish fry is a great way to help your family remember that they are part of a larger community, a group of Catholics who sacrifice, fast, and abstain during the season of penance and preparation. Typically, parishes have a price per family, so if you're one of those Catholics with a van load of kids, you could be in for a deal! If you have teenagers, the all-you-can-eat offers work out pretty great budget wise.

One question is which fish fry is the giant among them? The parish serving fish tacos? fried catfish? all-you-can-eat shrimp Alfredo? You have six Fridays to work with; why not try them all?

There are plenty of other ways for families to pull together to fast or abstain during Lent. The parish fish fry aside, you can give up going out to eat. Or maybe give up a certain type of food everyone enjoys at home. You can give up screens on certain days of the weeks or times of the day (or altogether, if you're the brave and adventurous type). These are just a few ideas.

Even young children can participate by fasting from screen time or from a particular toy they are obsessed with at the moment. As they get older, they can begin to engage in this aspect of the faith by fasting from one snack time during the day or from a sweet treat after dinner. Children appreciate feeling connected to something bigger—their family, their community, their faith. When we give them an opportunity to join in a fast, even in a small way, it can leave a big impression on them.

Families can take it to the next level and give up something like complaining, gossiping, or being late. But if a family is going to give up a bad habit together for Lent, everyone has to be accountable to everyone else. This can be difficult, mostly because it requires humility. When the kids gripe about having to eat green beans at dinner, parents will need to remind them that the family agreed to give up complaining. Likewise, children have to be empowered to call out parents for walking in the door and unloading negativity, complaints, and frustration after a brutal day on the job.

Having it work both ways can be challenging, but it can also be beautiful. It can give children a feeling of being part of something bigger, part of God's plan for their entire family's growth in holiness. It can also help ensure that the momentary sacrifices stick with your children long into their lives, motivating them when they have families of their own.

No matter what the family gives up or takes on, it's important to remind yourself that nothing is ever perfect, and we all need to cut each other a little slack from time to time. Sure, your kids might be excited to give up playing with their favorite toy on Ash Wednesday, but come Saturday, they might want it back. Cut them—and yourself—some slack. It isn't good to push our kids (or ourselves) to the brink over maintaining what we've given up for Lent. If we've given up chocolate, but everything in life seems to be falling to pieces and a little fun-sized chocolate candy is the only thing that's going to help us make it through, that's okay. Eat the chocolate, and vow to get back on the horse tomorrow. And when it comes to kids and Lent, remember: they're kids, after all, and we have to allow them space to do their best and start over if they need to.

To Cheat or Not to Cheat?

Which brings us to the next all-important question when it comes to Catholics and Lenten sacrifices: can you "cheat" on Sundays?

The United States Conference of Catholics Bishops includes a little bit about this on their website's question-and-answer section:

> Q. So does that mean that when we give something up for Lent, such as candy, we can have it on Sundays?
> A. Apart from the prescribed days of fast and abstinence on Ash Wednesday and Good Friday, and the days of abstinence every Friday of Lent, Catholics have traditionally chosen additional penitential practices for the whole Time of Lent. These practices are disciplinary in nature and often more effective if they are continuous, i.e., kept on Sundays as well. That being said, such practices are not regulated by the Church, but by individual conscience.[18]

Like a good parent, the Church gives us advice and then leaves it up to us to decide. But is there biblical evidence for allowing ourselves to celebrate Sundays by indulging *just a little bit*?

In the Gospel of Matthew, we find something that may be a defense for the position of a Sunday cheat day: "Can the wedding guests mourn as long as the bridegroom is with them? The days will come when the bridegroom is taken away from them, and then they will fast" (9:15). On Sundays we celebrate the death and resurrection of Our Lord. Each Sunday is a celebration, and as such, we should be feasting rather than fasting.

But the choice to feast or fast is nothing more than a preference. We shouldn't feel as though we're better than someone else because we keep on keeping on with our Lenten fast on the Lord's Day. Instead, let's embrace the diversity of opinions when the Church allows them. After all, chocolate on Sundays *does* sound nice, doesn't it?

Remembering the Reason for the Season

No matter what we give up, how often we abstain from meat, or whether we indulge on Sundays, we have to stay focused on the reason for the Lenten season. It's easy to fall into the trap whereby fasting and abstinence become ends in themselves rather than means to an end. We have to remember, and help our children to understand, that fasting and abstinence mean *absolutely nothing* apart from the sacrifice of Christ. Our sacrifices, however big or small, have no value unless they are connected to his sacrifice on the cross. We give something up for Lent because he gave everything up on Calvary. We abstain from meat on Fridays to help us remember that he embraced all the pain and suffering of the crucifixion for us on Good Friday. We sacrifice because he did.

If we can stay focused on that, our families will have a successful and holy Lenten observance no matter how successful we are at giving something up. We will make a conscious effort to allow Jesus to guide us during this all-important season of penance and sacrifice, and that will make all the difference.

Almsgiving

The *Catechism of the Catholic Church* says that "giving alms to the poor is a witness to fraternal charity: it is also a work of justice pleasing to God" (CCC, 2462). Along with prayer and fasting, almsgiving is one of the three pillars of Lent. And Jesus has a lot to say about almsgiving and giving to the needy.

For starters, consider this: "Sell your belongings and give alms" (Luke 12:33). Or consider the Beatitudes: "I was hungry and you gave me food, I was thirsty and you gave me drink, a stranger and you welcomed me, naked and you clothed me, ill and you cared for me, in prison and you visited me" (Matthew 25:35-36). Jesus isn't just giving random examples here of what his followers should be doing. The Beatitudes list the things demanded of the followers of Jesus if they're going to make the cut for heaven. To those who fail to do these works of mercy, he says, "Depart from me, you accursed, into the eternal fire prepared for the devil and his angels" (25:41).

The bottom line is that we must dig deep and give freely to our sisters and brothers who have not. When we give financially, we should be generous; when we give goods such as clothing or household items, those should be in excellent condition. No matter what we give, Lent offers an opportunity to be attentive to and help meet the needs of others.

Giving to a Charity as a Family

We handle our Lenten giving in the same way as our Advent giving—by working with our children to select a charity that means something to them and that touches the lives of all the members of the family. Young kids have almost no idea what various amounts of money mean, so we put the donation in more practical terms, to help them grasp what the family will need to sacrifice in order to help.

When we tell our kids we're giving $100 to help those in need, they say something like "That's nice" and then go about their business. When we switch it up a bit and tell them we're giving away two-weeks' worth of grocery money—two-weeks' worth of the money we typically spend on all of our breakfasts, lunches, dinners, and snacks—it helps the amount to sink in. They can appreciate on a practical level what this sacrifice means for our family, especially as the menus start to involve a lot more beans and rice or that lablabi soup from Iraq.

Operation Rice Bowl

We discussed using Operation Rice Bowl recipes during Lent, but Operation Rice Bowl is primarily a way to donate money to help the needy through Catholic Relief Services, the international humanitarian aid arm of the Catholic community in the

United States. Catholic Relief Services has been running with this idea for quite a while. Back in 1975, Operation Rice Bowl kicked off at a few parishes in Pennsylvania. During the Lenten season, parishioners received a small cardboard box—a piggy bank of sorts—in which to stash their spare change and money they saved by giving up luxuries, such as going out to eat or that daily coffee at a nearby coffee shop. At the end of Lent, they brought the money they had collected back to their parish as an offering for those in need.

Within a year, the United States Conference of Catholic Bishops adopted Operation Rice Bowl as a national program, and one year after that, the USCCB voted to make it an official program of Catholic Relief Services. Decades later, parishioners across the United States eagerly await the Rice Bowl on Ash Wednesday. They happily put in money for others that they would have spent on themselves.

In the first forty years of the program, over $250 million has been raised to improve water conditions, develop farming programs, provide maternal and children's health and nutrition programs, improve education for children, and address other needs around the world. When kids contribute to the Rice Bowl during Lent, turning their bowls in at Mass as Lent wraps up, they have a tangible experience of what it means to practice self-denial in order to serve the needy.

Reaching into Your Closets, in addition to Your Wallet

Have you opened your kids' drawers lately? Better yet, have you opened your own?

If your home is anything like ours, you have somehow accumulated *way too much stuff*. Lent is the perfect time of year to take stock of what you have and honestly assess what you need. Does your five-year-old really need six pairs of jeans? Does your second-grader need four sweatshirts? Do you really need five pairs of dress shoes for work? How many baseball hats does one man need? Is it really necessary to have three purses, to make sure you're always matching your bag with your outfit?

It isn't easy to take stock of the things we have; after all, we *might* eventually need four scarves. But Peter Maurin, cofounder of the Catholic Worker Movement and friend of Dorothy Day, famously said, "The coat that hangs in your closet belongs to the poor."[21] That's the mindset we ought to have as we review our belongings. If our kids leave the nest with a proper understanding of the distinction between wants and needs, as well as a proper understanding of the importance of giving to help our sisters and brothers in need, we will have taught them a valuable lifelong lesson.

That Shirt with a Hole Isn't for the Poor

A not-often-discussed topic regarding donating items for the poor is the quality and condition of the items we give away. Sadly, when we go through our closets and household goods to set aside items for the Society of St. Vincent de Paul, we seem to reach for the items we would no longer wear or use ourselves. Dress shoes with a hole in the bottom, jackets with busted zippers, shirts that never fit right because they were cut oddly from the beginning. Choosing ill-fitting "painting clothes" to pass along to the poor doesn't quite hit the bar of abundant, sacrificial generosity that Jesus set for us.

When selecting items to give away, we should remember the dignity of all of God's children. No matter how little a person has, they deserve nice things just as much as everyone else.

Once again, the Catholic Worker Movement provides a great frame of reference for this. On the Catholic Worker website, an article by Jim Forest titled "Dorothy Day—A Saint for Our Age?" shares this story of the Servant of God:

> Tom Cornell tells the story of a donor coming into the New York house one morning and giving Dorothy a diamond ring. Dorothy thanked her for the donation and put it in her pocket without batting an eye. Later a certain demented lady came in, one of the more irritating regulars at the CW house, one of those people who make you wonder if you were cut out for life in a house of hospitality. I can't recall her ever saying "thank you" or looking like she was on the

141

edge of saying it. She had a voice that could strip paint off the wall. Dorothy took the diamond ring out of her pocket and gave it to this lady.

Someone on the staff said to Dorothy, "Wouldn't it have been better if we took the ring to the diamond exchange, sold it, and paid that woman's rent for a year?" Dorothy replied that the woman had her dignity and could do what she liked with the ring. She could sell it for rent money or take a trip to the Bahamas. Or she could enjoy wearing a diamond ring on her hand like the woman who gave it away. "Do you suppose," Dorothy asked, "that God created diamonds only for the rich?"[19]

Don't feel bad about throwing the shoes with holes in them into the trash. Give the nice ones to the poor.

That Local Parish Ministry

We are called to give of our treasure, indeed, but the Church also calls us to give of our time and talents during the season of Lent (and all year, for that matter). Plenty of ministries at your local parish need volunteers and support. Lent offers an opportunity to determine how much time you *actually* have available and to select a parish ministry that could use your help. And while you're at it, why not focus on finding a ministry where your children can help out as well?

Your parish bulletin and website list numerous possibilities. There's probably a group that helps clean the church, a group that gets things ready for Mass, a group that organizes

Eucharistic Adoration, people who volunteer to spend an hour with the Lord in Eucharistic Adoration (yes, your kids can do that too, as long as you brace yourself for how challenging it might be), and even groups that take prayer requests and intercede for them. Find something that works for your family, and chip in during the Lenten season.

NINE

IT TAKES A VILLAGE

Surrounding your family with other families living their faith

In her autobiography, *The Long Loneliness*, Servant of God Dorothy Day remarked, "We have all known the long loneliness and we have learned that the only solution is love and that love comes with community."[20] Being a Catholic family, and especially a Catholic family who takes the faith seriously, can be lonely. We are living in an extremely secular culture, and most people we encounter in the course of our day find our lifestyle a bit odd.

After all, as we've said, being a Catholic family in today's world is a seriously countercultural choice. We believe that marriage truly is "until death do us part." We oppose the horror of abortion. We tend to have more kids than most because of our stance against contraception. We believe in standing up for the oppressed, the poor, and the persecuted.

Sometimes we might want to give up rather than push on as a Catholic family. Wouldn't it be easier to go along to get along? Wouldn't it be better to go with the flow rather than risk losing friends because of our pro-life stance? It can feel that way, to be sure, but still we push on.

As Dorothy Day reminds us, we need community in order to overcome the loneliness in the long struggle of life. But where do we find that community in a world where people turn in on themselves and reach for the screen rather than actual human contact?

Catholics and the Village

When we were dating and then first married, the idea of *needing* to have Catholic friends didn't occur to us. Sure, it was nice to hang out with Catholics—we "got" each other—but we didn't feel a strong need for community. With the arrival of our first child, however, that need groaned within us.

We can attribute this, in part, to the fact that having children made us take our faith more seriously. When you have kids, you realize that they're watching you, observing to see if you're living an authentic life, if you practice what you preach. This awareness helped us strengthen our commitment to being Catholic.

The other part of realizing we needed Catholic friends came as we saw just how hard it is to raise children and start a family apart from a community. When we started our family, we lived in a southern California neighborhood where that sense of community was sorely lacking. Neighbors didn't say hi to each other, no one knew anyone else on the street, and everyone kept to themselves. Maybe this is the norm around the country, but we felt extremely isolated.

Who could we complain to when the baby wouldn't sleep for months on end? Who would watch our kids when we desperately needed to sneak out for the first date night in forever? We had a few friends like us, but we started to feel guilty relying on the same people over and over. We needed to embrace a community and be embraced back. The phrase "It takes a village" finally began to have meaning. We desperately craved community.

Settling in and Then Moving Away

We eventually found a nearby parish that felt like home. The priests were wonderful, there were young families who were serious about living as Catholics and raising their children in the faith, and we slowly met others who became our community. The parish began a group for young families while we were there—and it was just when we started to settle in that we decided to move.

Looking back, it was definitely the right thing to do. Karen's family lived in the Bay Area, and she was one of seven children. There was a lot more support for our young family up there than down south, where Tommy grew up as an only child. We cringed at the thought of moving, however. How were we going to leave this parish where we finally felt at home? How were we going to cast aside all the work we had done to engage in a community that could support us and that we could support?

In the end, the pull of being close to Karen's family and having our children grow up around aunts, uncles, and loads of cousins was just too appealing. We packed up, moved north, and started our new life.

Although it was good to have Karen's family nearby, there when we needed them, it was terrifying to try to find and connect with a new community of friends and young families. Things came together quickly, however, when we visited a parish we were trying out for the first time. We found a flyer in the back of the church for a toddler play group, open to all comers and held once per week at the parish. Karen went to the group with the kids, and we were almost instantly connected to Catholic families like us. We felt so blessed. The connections we made in this community helped give us the support we needed to carry on.

At the Same Time . . .

We only lived in that town for about a year, renting a small place that cost way too much. When we felt ready to buy a home of our own, we knew that staying in that city was unrealistic. We shifted our sights one town over, to a more reasonably priced area (if you can consider the Bay Area of California to be reasonably priced in any way). We bought a house in a quiet neighborhood with good public schools. We felt as if God was guiding us to the right place at the right time, but once again we faced the task of finding and settling into a new parish.

Going to a new parish for the first time can feel like moving to a new school as a kid. Everyone seems to know each other;

everyone seems to know the ins and outs, the details and history of the parish—everyone except you. It's unnerving to go to coffee and donuts after Mass, see everyone socializing, and feel too uncomfortable to join in. But as our family continued to grow and we continued to welcome more children, we put our uneasiness aside as the need intensified to fill the long loneliness with a supportive community of like-minded families.

As before, God didn't disappoint. We met a family and became such close friends that it felt as if we had known each other all along.

There's something so special about the sense of belonging, that sense that you aren't alone. Catholic parishes offer the answer to the need to belong if we're brave enough to look below the surface.

But It Didn't Come That Easy

Looking back, we can be tempted to think that the process was smooth, that we stepped automatically into community. That's not true. Knowing we needed community around us, we took steps to get involved and meet others, which wasn't easy.

At our first parish in southern California, we joined that young family group that was getting off the ground. It was nice to get to know families we had seen at Mass but never had an opportunity to meet. As we continued on, we tried to attend church functions as a family. We went to the parish welcoming nights, pancake breakfasts, and other parish events as a way of getting involved and getting to know others outside of the awkward hand-holding during the Our Father. We also joined some of the small groups at the parish. There was a lot of "work" involved in building that community.

What if none of these groups and events exist where you are?

If you've been in a Catholic parish for any length of time, you know what happens when you suggest that the parish start a particular group that might be helpful for parishioners. "That's a great idea," a pastor or parish leader will say. "Go start it!"

If you're like us, that idea is pretty terrifying. But if you find at least one other person willing to help you pull the idea together, it can become a reality and a great blessing for you and for other parishioners. If you feel that something is missing at your parish, chances are you're not the only one.

Of course, it can be difficult to make something like this happen. Bumps in the road can lead to rethinking the idea and questioning if it was worth pursuing, if anyone actually has any interest in the idea, and if this is what God wants you to do. Be brave, push on, and wait it out long enough to see if the idea fruit.

Hospitality: The Forgotten Virtue

Our Protestant sisters and brothers have much to teach Catholics about the importance and value of good fellowship. When it comes to hanging around and getting to know each other, our Protestant friends have us beat. If we Catholics would step out of our comfort zones and make efforts to meet people, we could build the kind of communities we long for.

And not just meet other people but be truly present to them, getting to know their joys, their sorrows, their dreams, and their struggles. If we did this even over something as simple as donuts and coffee, our parishes could become the kind of communities that will help to change the world.

You've Got a Friend

One bad habit we constantly have to fight against is looking at other people at Mass and thinking about how good they must have it.

"Look, she's so put together; she must have things so easy."

"They only have one kid; must be nice."

"That's a pretty nice car they're driving off in. I'll bet they're happy."

We look at our own sufferings and trials and close ourselves off to others, imagining that we're the only ones hurting, the only ones broken. And so we're left lonely, left to suffer alone in our darkness and trial.

The only way to break this is to reach out and get to know people—like, *really* get to know people. We will only open ourselves up to getting the support and community we need by allowing ourselves to be vulnerable and present to others who are making themselves vulnerable. Once we do, we realize that every other person at Mass is, in some way, suffering and broken—just like us.

Our parishes are filled with people who feel like outsiders in our Church. Even though the Church as a whole goes to great lengths to be welcoming to anyone and everyone, there are many who people just don't feel that welcoming atmosphere when they head into Mass on a Sunday morning. From the Catholics with disabilities to Catholics who have experienced divorce; to single parents; to converts who come to Mass despite their spouses staying home; to Catholic couples facing the silent pain of infertility, child death, or miscarriage; to Catholics with mental illness; to Catholics who have thoughts of suicide in the midst of hopelessness: *we are one body*. When one member of the body is left feeling unwelcome, *we are all unwelcome*.

Be willing to be a friend, support, and Catholic lifeline to others. We all need that. We all need the simple joys of laughter and easy companionship too. And when it comes to dealing with hard times, the more we take the time to get to know each other on a deep and personal level, the more we will understand others and feel understood. Those we encounter may have walked in our shoes at some point or may be walking in them right now, even though we don't realize it.

The great St. Teresa of Avila once said, "We always find that those who walked closest to Christ were those who had to bear the greatest trials."[22] It is only through walking that walk and bearing those trials together with others that we can ever hope to come to the end of our journey ready to enter the kingdom of heaven.

But I'm an Introvert

These ideas are all well and good, but what are you supposed to do if you're an introvert? What if the simple idea of just saying hi to someone makes you break out in hives?

It isn't easy to reach out to someone, even if you've just attended Mass together, have kids the same age, or seem to have interests in common. We all have memories of being rejected, which can get in the way when we want to reach out. Maybe you were rejected when asking someone to the high school Sadie Hawkins dance, for example, or maybe you were told to "get lost" as a kid when you were looking for someone to play with. Here again, it's important to remember that most people have similar experiences and may feel the same way.

Whatever is holding us back—whether we're self-conscious, or have been rejected in the past, or are too entranced by our glowing screens—we *have* to get back to engaging with people. Pope St. John Paul II was always very attentive to the people he met—when he was with someone, he was really with them, wholly present to them. We don't seem to have many interactions like that, but there's no reason we can't.

If we want to restore a world where people care about each other and pay attention to each other, *we* have to be the ones willing to make that change. *We* have to push through our uneasiness and begin to engage with people in an open and honest way.

It starts with us. Leave your phone in your pocket, and force yourself to be truly present to another person. It will take effort at first but gets easier over time, as we finally start to create the village that will be a source of joy and friendship and will help all of us get through the ups and downs of life.

CONCLUSION

When we were preparing to welcome our first child into the world, we wanted to make sure we did all the right things. We went to the library and checked out all the books about parenting and babies, we strapped the car seat into the car *months* before the due date, and we took meticulous notes while on the walking tour of the labor and delivery unit of our local hospital. We wanted to be ready for *anything* that parenthood could throw at us. And yes, we were terrified we'd make a mistake.

Once our son showed up, we tried to do everything right—to the point of making ourselves crazy. We *only* gave him organic food; we *only* put him down to sleep on his back, even after he could roll over with ease; we seriously restricted his use of a pacifier; and so on, because we were told all of those things would ruin him for life. We didn't realize that we were ruining our own lives.

As with most parents, we relaxed as we had another child and even more so when we had another. Eventually, we realized that parents and families need to do what is right and what is best for *them*, rather than trying to fit their children and family into a nice little box based on the answers found on parenting websites or in self-help books.

This attitude is even more important when it comes to living out and handing on the Catholic faith. In today's social media world, where everyone seems to post about how they have it all together with barely any effort, it can be tempting to do whatever it takes to keep up with the family in the next pew. We want our kids to know all their prayers before they can walk, to sit quietly and pay attention during Mass, to learn the essentials of the faith by the time they get to kindergarten. We want the peace that comes with a nightly family Rosary, the joy that comes with having cupcakes fresh from the oven to celebrate St. Patrick's Day, and the consistency that comes with daily Mass with all the kids in tow.

And we're terrified that if we don't manage to pull all of this off, our kids will flee from the Church as soon as they turn eighteen.

If there's one message we hope readers take away from this book, it's that everything is going to be okay. God is in control, and it is in abandoning ourselves to his providence that we will find peace and happiness, even when he seems to be asleep in the boat as the storm rages on.

Our families are all different. We have different needs, different tastes, and different amounts of energy after dealing with fifteen meltdowns while trying to get something more nutritious than cold cereal on the table for dinner.

Everything is going to be okay. He is in control.

Rather than scrolling through Facebook or reading the latest post from the blogging Catholic Super Parent, we need to reflect on *our* family and do what's best for *us*. No one knows your family better than you do. Rather than feeling constantly stressed out about our inability to do it all, we need to find the peace that comes with knowing that Jesus is ready to meet us where we're at. He'll come to us in those moments when we're most tired, on those days when we're most overwhelmed, and at our darkest points. He's waiting for us to turn toward the crucifix, let out a deep sigh, and say nothing more than, "Jesus, I trust in you."

He'll do the rest.

Endnotes

1. Clare Anderson and Joanna Bogle, *John Paul II, Man of Prayer: The Spiritual Life of a Saint* (Herefordshire, England: Gracewing Publishing, 2014).

2. United States Conference of Catholic Bishops, "The Two Shall Become One: The Sacrament of Reconciliation and Marriage," http://www.usccb.org/prayer-and-worship/sacraments -and-sacramentals/penance/sacrament-reconciliation -married-persons-examination-of-conscience.cfm.

3. Vatican II, *Lumen Gentium,* Dogmatic Constitution on the Church, 11 , November 21, 1964, http://www.vatican.va/ archive/hist_councils/ii_vatican_council/documents/vat-ii_ const_19641121_lumen-gentium_en.html.

4. Pope Francis twitter, August 23, 2018, https://twitter.com/ pontifex/status/1032590779951271936?lang=en.

5. Archbishop Charles Chaput, foreword to Dominican Sisters of St. Cecilia, *A Short Guide to Praying as a Family: Growing Together in Faith and Love Each Day* (Charlotte, NC: St. Benedict Press, 2015).

6. Vatican II, *Lumen Gentium,* Dogmatic Constitution on the Church, no. 11.

7. Pope John Paul II, Apostolic Exhortation *Redemptoris Custos* on the Person and Mission of St. Joseph in the Life of Christ and of the Church, August 15, 1989, nos. 22, 24, quoting Pope Paul VI, Discourse of March 19, 1969, http://w2.vatican.va/ content/john-paul-ii/en/apost_exhortations/documents/hf_jp- ii_exh_15081989_redemptoris-custos.html.

8. Pope Benedict XVI, General Audience, February 22, 2006, w2.vatican.va/content/benedict-xvi/en/audiences/2006/ documents/hf_ben-xvi_aud_20060222.html.

9. St. Padre Pio, Letter to Annita, July 15, 1913, as quoted by Oleada Joven, "St. Padre Pio on Listening to Your Guardian Angel," May 17, 2015, https://aleteia.org/2015/05/17/st-padre-pio-on-listening-to-your-guardian-angel/.

10. Chapter 7, "Preparing for Christmas." USCCB, "Advent 2018," usccb.org/prayer-and-worship/liturgical-year/advent/.

11. USCCB, "About Advent Wreaths," usccb.org/prayer-and-worship/liturgical-year/advent/about-advent-wreaths.cfm.

12. Lino Lozza, "The Christmas Tree: Legends, Traditions, History," *L'Osservatore Romano,* January 5, 2005, 10, ewtn.com/library/chistory/xmastree.htm.

13. St. Augustine, quoted by Carolyn Berghuis, "The Power of Fasting Part I," A Catholic Moment, acatholic.org/friday-2-12-16-the-power-fasting/.

14. St. Thomas Aquinas, quoted by Berghuis, Ibid.

15. St. Jane Frances de Chantal, Letter to Mother Marie-Adrienne Ficher, 1627, as quoted in Shawn Madigan, ed., *Mystics, Visionaries, and Prophets: A Historical Anthology of Women's Spiritual Writings* (Minneapolis: Fortress Press, 1998), 283.

16. Pope Benedict XVI, Message for Lent 2009, w2.vatican.va/content/benedict-xvi/en/messages/lent/documents/hf_ben-xvi_mes_20081211_lent-2009.html, cf. Pope John Paul II, *Veritatis Splendor,* 21.

17. USCCB, "Fast & Abstinence," usccb.org/prayer-and-worship/liturgical-year/lent/catholic-information-on-lenten-fast-and-abstinence.cfm.

18. USCCB, "Questions and Answers about Lent and Lenten Practices," http://www.usccb.org/prayer-and-worship/liturgical-year/lent/questions-and-answers-about-lent.cfm.

19. Jim Forest, "Dorothy Day—Saint for Our Age?" Catholic Worker, http://jimandnancyforest.com/2011/10/writings-of-dorothy-day/.

20. Dorothy Day, *The Long Loneliness* (San Francisco: HarperCollins, 1952), 286.

21. Dorothy Day, "More About Holy Poverty. Which Is Voluntary Poverty," *The Catholic Worker*, February 1945, 4, http://www.catholicworker.org/dorothyday/articles/150.pdf.

22. St. Teresa of Avila, *Complete Works St. Teresa Of Avila*, Burns & Oats, New York, NY, 345.